MS-DOS
for beginners

Helmut Tornsdorf

Abacus
A Data Becker Book

Third Printing, March 1990
Printed in U.S.A.

ISBN   1-55755-061-1

Table of Contents

Introduction

Congratulations, you're now the proud owner of a PC. Now you need to learn the basics of your personal computer and MS-DOS. If you've never heard the term MS-DOS before, you've bought the right book. Because using a computer can be confusing to the beginner, most new users wish they had an experienced friend or teacher to help them through the first steps of using a PC.

This book is here to help. We don't have any more time available than others, but we felt that our own experiences would be of assistance to you. This book should put you on the way to knowing your computer more quickly and with less effort, while enjoying the process.

Before we start, we want to tell you the structure of this book, and how it will help you feel comfortable computing:

1. Step by step learning. You won't learn everything about a particular command at once. We start with the simpler aspects of a command. Once you've learned these aspects, we go on to more complex capabilities. There will be some repetition, but this is important in the beginning stages of any learning process.

2. Reference. After working with us step by step through your new equipment and its capabilities, you will occasionally want to look up something. The alphabetized glossary at the end of this book will help you easily find command words. This reference section means this book will be of use to you long after you've passed beginner's status.

3. Practical experience. You'll get actual "hands-on" experience working with commands. There's only so much book learning you can do; we show you how to apply your knowledge.

Organization   The organization of this book is a result of a step by step examination of the requirements. The following is a quick overview of what you can expect to learn from the individual chapters of this book.

Chapter 1   This chapter introduces the new terms MS-DOS and PC. You'll learn what these terms mean and what they have to do with you. This chapter also helps the user gain experience in MS-DOS quickly. Exercises include creating backup copies of the original MS-DOS disk and instructing MS-DOS to perform simple tasks.

Chapter 2   This chapter introduces commands that display the *directory* (contents) of a disk on the screen, and even send these contents to a printer.

Chapter 3   This chapter takes you through the process of preparing a new disk for accepting data, or formatting. In addition, you'll learn the basics of disk files—how to create, rename, open, copy, print and even destroy them.

Chapter 4   Here we introduce you to some simple utilities and shortcuts. You'll learn how to use a single command for several files at once, and how to save retyping commands using the function keys. We also show you more information about disk directories.

Chapter 5   This chapter shows you how to save yourself the trouble of entering the same sequence of commands every time you turn on your PC. You'll learn about the AUTOEXEC.BAT (AUTOEXECute BATch) file, how it controls the computer when you turn it on, and how you can create your own AUTOEXEC.BAT file.

Chapter 6   This chapter discusses the text editor EDLIN which comes with most MS-DOS packages. You'll learn how to edit the AUTOEXEC.BAT file described earlier using EDLIN. As a bonus, working with EDLIN gives you general knowledge about text editors and word processors.

Chapter 7   This chapter shows you how to create subdirectories, which can help keep floppy disks and hard disks organized. You'll also read about some advanced areas of MS-DOS.

Chapter 8   If you only have one disk drive, this chapter shows you how to have your PC simulate a second disk drive, without the added expense. We'll show you how to prepare *bootable* disks (i.e., disks that you can use to start up your PC). Finally, you'll learn more about batch files, and how they can make your sessions on a PC more productive.

Chapter 9   This chapter lists the most "common" errors, and what steps you can take to resolve these errors, when possible.

Glossary   The glossary at the end of this book provides a brief, intense list of important concepts and procedures. Again, this reference will be valuable to you long after you've finished reading this book.

We hope you'll have as much fun learning MS-DOS as we had writing about it.

H. Tornsdorf   November 1987

1.   Getting started

You probably had the same experience we had some time ago when we became involved with the PC for the first time. We met people who were very familiar with the equipment, while that same equipment was new to us. They often used the buzzword MS-DOS, and we never asked what it meant. We knew that this MS-DOS thing was somehow important to the PC.

When we turned on a PC for the first time, someone finally said that we had to insert the MS-DOS disk to go any farther. So, let's answer the burning question:

1.1   What is MS-DOS?

MS-DOS is the abbreviation for MicroSoft Disk Operating System. Microsoft Corporation manufactures MS-DOS. A disk operating system does just what its name suggests—controls disk commands.

Computers speak a different language than us. They think exclusively in numbers. Actually, they think in zeros and ones, or in the *binary system*. People could probably think in binary, but we need an *interface* or bridge that allows the computer to understand the user, and vice versa. This interface should allow the user to enter commands in English form that the computer can *execute* (use). These commands are actually short programs which the computer executes in its own way.

The basic functions of the operating system include:

•   Testing characters and numbers entered from the keyboard. The operating system determines whether these characters make up a command which must be executed, or data that must be stored (e.g., text).

- Store data on disk.

- Recall stored data from disk.

- Provide a name to a *file*, or set of data on a disk.

- Allow the renaming, copying or deletion of a file.

- Recognize date and time and store this data in files.

- Lots more.

As you can see, not much can happen in a computer without an operating system.

Let's look at Microsoft, the MS in MS-DOS. This corporation manufactures computer programs and operating systems. In August of 1981, IBM (International Business Machines) introduced the first IBM PC, a computer intended for use by an individual (hence the PC, for Personal Computer). IBM needed an operating system for the new computer, and favored a proposal written by Microsoft Corporation.

MS-DOS has undergone many changes since 1981. This operating system exists in many forms, or versions. For example, Version 4.0 of MS-DOS has just hit the market as we write this. The most common version is currently Version 3.3. Versions of MS-DOS exist from Version 1.0 (1981) to Version 4.0, with many versions in between. The higher the number, the newer the version of MS-DOS.

The first version (DOS 1.0) came packaged with the PC when you bought it from IBM. In those days the PC could only handle single sided disks. DOS Version 1.1 changed this. In March 1983, IBM introduced the PC/XT, which included a hard disk drive for additional storage. This early hard disk could store up to 10 megabytes (over 10 million characters). Since the larger number of files that could be stored on a hard disk would be harder to maintain and find, DOS 2.0 included the option of adding subdirectories (directories within directories).

DOS 2.1, introduced in March 1984, added country-specific features. The date could be entered in either European (day.month.year) or English-American format (month-day-year). This version of MS-DOS was delivered to IBM. The manufacturers who were selling IBM PC *clones* (copies) received DOS Version 2.11.

The end of 1984 saw the release of Versions 3.0 and 3.1. They were capable of operating the new, bigger brother of the PC, the AT (see the glossary at the end of this book). The AT could handle denser disk formats and larger hard disk drives.

The current version being shipped by most PC clone manufacturers is MS-DOS 3.2. Since this is the version packaged with most PC compatibles, this is the version we'll be using throughout this book.

In the meantime, MS-DOS versions 3.3 and 4.0 have been released, but they offer no significant innovations that will interest the beginner.

We gave you this quick history of DOS to show you its evolution, and to show you that more than one version of DOS exists. There's a second and even more important reason. It's possible that you have a version of MS-DOS other than Version 3.2. If so, you should know the following important information:

- You cannot intermix versions of DOS. That is, if you boot your computer with DOS Version 3.2, the computer requests a version 3.2 disk whenever it needs to recall any on-disk commands.

- MS-DOS is *upwardly compatible*. This means that all programs which ran under DOS 2.11 will also run with DOS 3.2. The other way doesn't hold true, however. If you have an older version of DOS, learn what you can about the newer commands—they could be useful later when you finally do buy a more current DOS version.

In short, MS-DOS is an operating system. This operating system gives the computer basic instructions about disk and file management, and allows communication between the computer and user.

1.2   PC close-up

Let's examine our equipment more closely. This examination must be kept generalized. So many PC compatible computers are on the market, in so many different configurations, that we can't single out one particular model. However, most of the descriptions in this section apply to your PC.

1.2.1   What is a PC?

The terms PC and personal computer once applied to machines that now carry the label *home computer*. Some of the present day home computers actually pack more power and capabilities than the original 1981 IBM PC. Nowadays, however, PC refers to IBM and IBM-compatible computer systems used by individuals, either at home or in the workplace.

The important distinction between the home computer and the PC lies in *compatibility*. This means that the computer's basic appearance and brand name are unimportant. A PC compatible can be manufactured by a small company in Minneapolis, or a huge Asian conglomerate. The main requirement of a PC compatible is that it be able to execute all the programs that execute on a true IBM PC. Slight differences occur from computer to computer. Some of these changes actually improve on the genuine IBM product, yet these same changes may mean that some software won't run on some compatibles.

In any case, a PC by our definition uses the MS-DOS operating system, and can process data created by other compatible PCs.

Let's look at the individual components of the system. We've made the description of each part as non-technical and as general as possible. When any technical terms appear, we give general definitions.

1.2.2   The computer itself

The basis of a PC system is a metal or plastic case about the size of a drawer. Usually this case has one or more horizontal slots in front of it. The front of your PC may also have a power light which tells you the PC is on when lit; lights next to the horizontal slots; and a separate light the same color as the lights next to the slots.

The box contains the computer itself. This consists of a set of electronic circuit boards which hold a number of *chips* (black rectangular components). These chips include the circuitry which drives the PC, *memory* (electronic storage areas) and other items.

1.2.3   Data storage

The horizontal slot or slots on the front of the case are important to us. These are the doors to the *disk drives*, which are used for reading and writing data to and from *floppy disks*. These disk drives handle two different formats (sizes): 5-1/4" and 3-1/2" formats. These disks and disk handling will be discussed below.

Hard disks are becoming more popular. Usually they are mounted inside the computer cabinet. Unlike floppy disks, hard disks retain much more information. However, hard disks cannot be exchanged, are more expensive, and are sensitive to shock and other outside influences. The hard disk is the only choice for storing larger amounts of data. The average hard disk holds 20 megabytes (over 20 million characters, or about 10,000 typewritten pages).

1.2.4   The monitor

Reading, storing and processing of data would not be very effective, or even possible, if the data could not be displayed. PCs use monitors for data display. The monitor, which is often *monochrome* (single-color, usually amber or green), normally sits on top of the PC case.

1.2.5   The keyboard

The keyboard of the PC allows the user to enter data. The PC keyboard looks basically like a typewriter keyboard, but has a few more keys. The keyboard arrangement can differ from machine to machine.

We use a special notation to help distinguish keys from regular text. When we talk about a key, we place the key name between less than and greater than characters. For example, <3> represents the key with the number 3 embossed on it.

Function keys   The most obvious difference from a typewriter is the set of keys numbered from <F1> to <F10>. These *function keys* perform different functions, depending on the program in use on the computer. MS-DOS uses these function keys as well—but more on this later.

Keypad

Most keyboards include a square block of numbered keys. This block, or *numeric keypad*, allow fast number entry similar to a calculator keyboard. Like the function keys, the use of the numeric keypad varies from program to program.

Arrow keys

Some of these numbered keys also have arrows embossed on them, with each arrow pointing in a different direction (usually the <8>, <4>, <6> and <2> keys). These are the *arrow keys* or *cursor keys*, which allow the user to move the *cursor* in certain programs. This cursor marks the current location on the screen. If you press a key, a character appears at the current cursor location.

<Enter>

Three keys in particular are vital to our study. The <Enter>, <Return> or <↵> key is the one you'll probably use most often. Pressing this key on a typewriter advances the paper to the next line. This also occurs in some PC programs. However, the primary function of the <Enter> key is data entry. That is, the <Enter> key tells the computer to store or execute the text entered up to the <Enter> key. The user can edit commands before pressing the <Enter> key. Even though the terms <Enter> and <Return> are used interchangeably, we use <Enter> throughout this book.

<Ctrl>

The <Ctrl> key is an abbreviation for Control. It acts as an important part of sending *control characters*, used in telecommunication, text editing and other features. DOS uses the <Ctrl> key a great deal, as we'll soon see.

<Alt>

The other key bears the legend <Alt>, which is short for Alternate. Like <Ctrl>, <Alt> operates in conjunction with other keys to produce many additional commands and inputs (more on this later).

We use a certain set of names to describe certain keys. Your computer's keys or manual may use different names. Here are some different notations for the more frequently used keys:

Key	Keyboard appearance
Alt	ALT, Alt, Alternate
End	END, End
Home	HOME, Home
Ctrl	Control, CTRL, Ctrl
Del	DELETE, Delete
Ins	INS, Insert, Ins
Enter	Enter, RETURN, ↵, ↵
Esc	ESCAPE, Escape
Backspace	Backspace, ←
Shift	SHIFT, ⇑
Tab	TAB, ⊢ →⊣
PgUp	PageUp, PgUp
PgDn	PageDn, PgDn
CapsLock	CAPS, Caps Lock, CAPS LOCK
Scroll Lock	SCROLL LOCK, Scroll Lock
NumLock	NUM LOCK, Num Lock
PrtSc	Print Screen, PRTSC, PrtSc

Keyboard notations

1.2.6   The mouse

Your PC may have another device for entering data other than the keyboard. A *mouse* is a small box about the size of a very overweight mouse, connected to the PC through a cable. Mice control cursor movement on the screen through the user movement. An average mouse has a ball poking out underneath it. When you place the mouse on a table with the ball touching the table top, and you move the mouse, the cursor moves on the monitor screen. Many programs make use of the mouse. You won't need a mouse for this book.

1.2.7   The printer

PCs can be used without printers, but you'll find very few PCs without printers. They're useful for printing letters, disk listings, and more. A printer must be properly connected to the PC. Otherwise, the printer won't print data, at best.

1.3   Your first session

Now that you know about a few basic terms, we can turn on the PC and get some hands-on experience. You'll recall our three-step process mentioned in the Introduction:

1.)   Step by step learning

2.)   Reference

3.)   Practical experience

We'll follow this process throughout the book.

As the old law says, if it can go wrong, it will. You may run into problems as you're going through the processes of this book. To avoid panic, read the instructions carefully before performing the hands-on experience. If the computer responds with error messages, check Chapter 9 at the end of this book for some solutions to common errors.

1.3.1   Switching on the PC

You can now *power-up* (turn on) your computer. If possible, turn on the monitor first—this seems to be better for the system. Now turn on the computer.

The monitor displays a few lines of text describing the manufacturer of the device's internal system. Our screen looks like this (yours may look different—don't panic):

```
Phoenix ROM BIOS Ver 2.27
Copyright (c) 1984,1985,1986 Phoenix Technologies Ltd
All Rights Reserved
YANGTECH.INC
```

At some point the computer may count quickly through a set of numbers. This *memory test* checks to see how much memory (electronic workspace) is available. Usually this number lies between 256K (kilobytes, or thousands of bytes) and 640K. One kilobyte equals 1,024 bytes. A byte is the equivalent of a character.

If your PC only has floppy disk drives (i.e., you have no hard disk), the PC eventually displays a message which may look something like this:

```
Non-system disk or disk error
Replace and press any key to continue
```

Hard disk

If you have a PC with a hard disk, the computer may load MS-DOS from the hard disk. If so, don't panic. Read on.

Look in the MS-DOS packaging (you either bought this package or the manufacturer was kind enough to supply it with your PC). Usually two disks come in this packaging:

1.)   MS-DOS, sometimes called the *system disk*.

2.)   *Utilities* (special programs to help programming and file management) and some version of the BASIC language.

The system disk should be clearly marked with a label saying MS-DOS, System Disk, Startup Disk, or something similar. This disk, as its name implies, contains the operating system proper. Look for the topmost disk drive (if you have more than one). We call this disk drive drive A:.

Disk handling

When handling disks, there's one rule you must follow: Don't touch any shiny parts! The 5-1/4" disks have openings which expose the material used to store data. Don't handle disks by these openings. If you have 3-1/2" disks, a metal or plastic guard protects this data storage material. You may see this material by sliding the guard aside, but don't touch.

Pick up the system diskette carefully (do not touch the recording material). Remove it from its envelope if there is one. Insert the disk in the drive using the instructions for your disk format:

5-1/4"

Look for the *write protect notch* (the square notch cut into one side of the disk). This notch should be to your left, and the large opening exposing the disk material should be farthest from you. If your system disk has no write protect notch, position the disk so that the disk label points toward you and the opening points away from you. Make sure that the lever above the disk drive is parallel with the disk opening (your drives may be different—check your user's manual). Slide the disk into the topmost horizontal slot shiny material first, and with the write protect notch to your left and the label toward you. Slide the disk in until it stops. Move the lever 90° down so that it blocks the disk drive

slot. The PC cannot read the disk if the drive isn't closed.
Press the requested key.

3-1/2"   Hold the disk so that the metal guard points away from you.
Look for a metal circle built into one side of the disk.
Position the disk so that this metal circle points toward the
floor. Slide the disk into the drive metal guard first. Gently
slide the disk until it seems to stop. Give the disk a push
until it locks firmly into place. Press the requested key.

Note: If you have a hard disk, and the PC has already loaded DOS
from there, no problem. Place your system disk in drive A:
according to the instructions listed above. Press and hold the
<Ctrl> and <Alt> keys. Now press the <Del> key while
holding down the other two keys. Release all three keys
after doing this. DOS will now boot from drive A:.

The PC should display information on the monitor screen about the
version of DOS in use. The PC may or may not also ask you for the
current date and time. If it doesn't ask you for date or time and just
displays A>, don't worry—your PC and DOS version may just work
this way. If your computer does ask for the current date, press the
<Enter> key. If it asks for the current time, just press the <Enter> key.

System prompt Finally an A> should appear on the screen. This A> represents the
system prompt, which indicates that the computer is now waiting for a
command. To the right of the command you'll see a blinking square—
the cursor.

If an error message appears instead of the prompt, switch off the PC.
Wait about ten seconds, turn it back on and try the whole process
again. If after several attempts the A> prompt still has not appeared,
and the PC keeps asking for a system disk, try the following:

• Make sure you've got the system disk in drive A:.

• Make sure you inserted the disk properly (see the insertion
directions above).

• Take the disks to the dealer for testing and replacement.

1.3.2   Commanding your PC

The goal of this book is to make you familiar with the use of MS-DOS and your computer. Thus, the commands you address to the computer have central significance. The following describes the *command syntax*, or the way you should enter commands:

When the system prompt A> appears, you can enter a command. The command syntax starts with a command name if the command can be executed directly from MS-DOS. The command name can often be an actual filename, a utility program, or the name of an application program you want to run (e.g., a word processor). MS-DOS accepts commands in either upper case or lower case letters. MS-DOS isn't case-sensitive. However, we'll display the commands throughout this book in upper case letters, to make them easily readable.

Once you enter the command word, this word may require some extra *parameters*. Parameters are additional instructions needed by some commands. These instructions control the type, source and destination of command execution. This book lists parameters as needed for commands. A command executes when you press the <Enter> key.

Important news for hard disk users: The dealer from which you bought your PC with a hard disk probably set up your hard disk for you. We've already said that it's great to have a hard disk, but for this book, we want you to use MS-DOS on floppy disks. Make sure that you, as a hard disk user, do the following as you read this book and work through the exercises:

•   Before you turn on your PC, place your MS-DOS system disk in drive A: (the main disk drive visible on the PC cabinet—probably the <u>only</u> disk drive visible). Turn on the PC with this disk in drive A:. Keep this disk in drive A: unless told otherwise by us.

•   The system prompt should always read A>. If it doesn't enter the following to make it so:

        A:<Enter>

Follow these rules to keep us all working at the same pace. If you disobey these rules, and use your hard disk for some of the DOS exercises, you could change some files that you shouldn't have changed.

1.4 Copying your DOS disks

The two disks which comprise MS-DOS are indispensable to the PC's operation. Our first hands-on task in MS-DOS will be to make *backup* (duplicate) copies of these disks, since they're so important. You'll need:

- Some blank disks

- Labels (should have been provided with the disks)

- A felt-tip pen (a fine point felt-tip pen—using regular markers makes the disk labels hard to read)

If you have no disks, don't do anything else with your PC. Remove any disks currently in the disk drive as follows:

5-1/4" Flip up the drive lever so that it lies parallel with the disk drive slot. Reach in and remove the disk.

3-1/2" Look for a button near the disk drive. Push this button to release the disk.

Turn off your computer and monitor. Now go to a software or computer store, or even a toy store, and buy some disks. Make sure that the disks you buy:

- Match the format of your PC (5-1/4" or 3-1/2")

- Are double-sided and double-density (the package should say something like DSDD)

- Are high quality (there may be a few different brands—look for a brand you might recognize, like Sony, Maxell, KAO, etc.)

Once you return from the store with your blank disks, you need to *write protect* your original disks. You can do this as follows:

5-1/4" Pick up your MS-DOS system disk (remember not to handle the shiny parts). Look for the *write protect notch* (the square notch cut into one side of the disk). If no write protect notch exists, disregard these instructions (compare the system disk with one of your new disks—these should have write-protect notches). Search in your package of new

14

disks; you should find a sheet of paper containing small adhesive-backed pieces of paper, about 1/2" x 3/4". These are *write protect tabs*. Take a write protect tab off the sheet and place it on the disk so that it covers the write protect notch. This protects the system disk from accidental erasure or overwriting. Cover the write protect on the second MS-DOS disk in the same manner.

3-1/2"   Pick up your MS-DOS system disk. Hold it so that the metal circle mentioned above faces you, and the metal guard points toward the floor. On the upper left corner of the disk you'll see a small piece of plastic set into the disk. This is the write protect. Take your fingernail or a pen and move the write protect to the opposite of its original location. You'll know the disk is write protected because you'll be able to see through this place on the disk—moving the write protect opens an actual hole in the disk. Write protect the other DOS disk in the same manner.

Insert your DOS system disk in drive A: (check the insertion instructions above if you don't remember how). Make sure the disk is securely in the drive—close the drive lever if you have a 5-1/4" disk. Turn on the monitor and computer. Wait for the DOS prompt. If DOS asks you for the correct date and time, just press the <Enter> key to bypass to the DOS prompt.

Now we're going to enter an MS-DOS command. Make sure that you enter the following exactly as written:

DISKCOPY

Editing errors   If you made a mistake, you can erase the incorrect characters and re-enter them. Look for a key marked either <Backspace> or <⇐> (we'll call this <Backspace> throughout this book). Press the <Backspace> key to delete all the characters to the left of the cursor. Enter the correct word again, so that the line looks like this including the DOS prompt:

A>DISKCOPY

DISKCOPY   This command invokes the disk copying program. Press the <Enter> key to execute the DISKCOPY command. The disk drive runs. Most versions of MS-DOS display the following line (yours may be different—follow the instructions on the screen):

```
Insert source diskette in Drive A:
Press any key when ready...
```

Leave the write protected system diskette inserted in drive A:. This is our *source* diskette. Press the <Enter> key again. The following message appears (the numbers change depending on the disk format):

```
Copying 40 (80) tracks
9 Sectors/Track, 2 Side(s)
```

Wait. The disk drive runs for a while. After a while a prompt similar to this appears:

```
Insert target diskette in Drive A:
Press any key when ready ...
```

Remove the system disk from the disk drive. Take one of the new diskettes out of the package. Insert it exactly as you inserted the original system disk. Press the <Enter> key. The following prompt or something like it appears on the screen:

```
Formatting diskette during copying
```

Formatting prepares a new disk so that it can accept data. After some time the following prompt appears:

```
Copy another diskette (Y/N)?
```

Press the <N> key and wait a moment. If the A> prompt doesn't appear almost immediately, press the <Enter> key. Look in the package of new disks for some blank labels. They are adhesive-backed pieces of paper. Write the words BACKUP SYSTEM on a label (you might want to include today's date as well). Remove the new disk from the drive. Remove the label you just wrote on and place it on the new disk.

Insert the new disk into drive A:. We'll be using this for our course of study. Put the original DOS disk in a plastic disk box and place it somewhere non-magnetic (a linen closet works well).

Take the original DOS disk out of your secure place for making backups only.

Summary   We learned how to write protect a disk to prevent accidental erasure of
                   data when copying.

                   We created a backup copy of the original MS-DOS diskette with the
                   help of the DISKCOPY command.

1.5   Configuring DOS

MS-DOS can be configured to your needs and the system's needs. This section shows you how to make the computer ask for the current date and time. These instructions may seem complex to you, but enter them just as they appear below. The result will be great, and we'll explain what you're doing as we go along.

Make sure that the backup you made of the MS-DOS system disk is in drive A:. Enter the following at the A> prompt (press the <Enter> key when the text tells you to press <Enter>). Be sure that you enter it exactly as it appears below:

```
COPY CON MYFILE.BAT<Enter>
```

COPY

The COPY command tells the PC to copy data from a source device to a target device, similar to the source and target disks used in the DISKCOPY command. The command sequence you just entered tells the PC to copy any data entered at the console (i.e., the keyboard) to a file named MYFILE.BAT. Don't worry about just what MYFILE.BAT is for now, just enter the line. The prompt won't reappear. The cursor just stands there blinking, waiting for you to enter more data. Any data you enter now will be written to the file MYFILE.BAT.

Enter the following:

```
VER<Enter>
```

This line tells the PC to display the current version of MS-DOS on the screen. Now enter the following:

```
DATE<Enter>
```

This line tells the PC to prompt the user for the current date in MM-DD-YY format. This format means, for example, that 04-16-87 is April 15, 1987. Enter the following:

```
TIME<Enter>
```

This line tells the PC to prompt the user for the current date in HH-MM-SS format. This format means, for example, that 13:55:00 is 1:55 p.m.

To end the file and store it on the disk, press and hold the <Ctrl> key. While holding the <Ctrl> key, press the <Z> key. This action, called pressing <Ctrl><Z>, saves the file to disk and returns you to the DOS prompt.

You have just created your first *batch file*. The MYFILE.BAT file executes when you enter its filename. DOS automatically loads and runs the file commands.

To test it out, make sure that the BACKUP SYSTEM disk is in drive A:. Enter the following at the DOS prompt (notice that you don't enter the .BAT):

MYFILE<Enter>

The computer executes the MYFILE.BAT file. First the PC displays the current version of MS-DOS. Next, it prompts you for the correct date. Enter the date in MM-DD-YY format. For example, enter 04-16-89 if today is April 16, 1989. Press <Enter>. The PC then prompts you for the current time. Enter the time in HH:MM:SS format. For example, enter 13:31:00 if the current time is 1:31 p.m. Press <Enter>. This information is stored in memory, and the system prompt appears.

The date and time are important. This information is added to disk files as they are updated, making it easier to keep track of current files.

1.6 Review

You've learned the following in this chapter:

- General knowledge of your PC's components.

- How to turn on your PC.

- How to handle disks.

- How to insert the DOS disk.

- How to make backup disks using the DISKCOPY command.

- How to instruct the PC to execute a group of simple commands.

2.   Short course in MS-DOS

The DISKCOPY command in Chapter 1 showed us that the PC will do what we tell it to do, provided that we enter the correct commands. Of course, we need to know the correct commands before we can enter them.

This chapter is designed to teach you the absolute basics of MS-DOS. This knowledge is more than most people need to know to use DOS. Set aside an evening's worth of time to work through this chapter; the result will be worth the time spent.

2.1   Basic DOS commands

The PC seemed more in control of us during DISKCOPY than we were of it. There's more to DOS than just copying disks, though. Let's learn some of the command words needed for minimum control of DOS.

2.1.1   Reaching an understanding

If your PC is off, insert your BACKUP SYSTEM disk in drive A: and turn on the PC according to the instructions listed in Chapter 1. Execute any tasks requested of the disk (e.g., date or time). Wait until the system prompt appears (A> or something similar).

Press down one of the <Shift> keys on the keyboard and enter the following text in upper case lettering. Release the <Shift> key after entering the text and press the <Enter> key:

HELLO<Enter>

The disk drive runs for a moment and the PC displays a message similar to the following:

Bad command or file name

The PC doesn't understand what you just entered. Enter the following to see what the PC does with equations:

1+1=<Enter>

The PC displays:

Bad command or file name

PCs are very dumb machines. The PC will only accept what it understands. For example, DISKCOPY is a DOS command known to the PC. Let's learn a few more DOS commands.

2.1.2   DATE and TIME

Enter the following text and press the <Enter> key. The text can be either in upper case or lower case lettering, since it makes no difference to the computer. During the course of this book we'll print the command words we want you to enter in upper case:

DATE<Enter>

The following message or something similar should appear on the screen:

Current date is Thu 2-13-86
Enter new date:

If another system date should appear, don't panic. This date changes with every version of MS-DOS.

Press the <Enter> key and the normal system prompt reappears. Enter the DATE command repeatedly and press <Enter> in response to the Enter new date: prompt. If no system date is entered, the PC retains the original date as "stamped" on the disk.

Pay strict attention to spaces between words. The PC is very, very choosy about the way commands are entered.

Enter the following:

DATE<Enter>

Again, the PC responds with:

Current date is Thu 2-13-86
Enter new date:

Notice the date structure. It appears in MM-DD-YY format. This means that to assign the current system date, you must enter the month as two digits (e.g., April appears as 04), the day as two digits (e.g., the sixteenth appears as 16) and the year as two digits (e.g., 1980 would be entered as 80).

Enter the following text exactly as it appears here. Separate each number with minus signs:

```
04-12-89<Enter>
```

The computer displays the system prompt. It doesn't look like anything happened. Enter the following:

```
DATE<Enter>
```

```
Current date is Wed 4-12-89
Enter new date:
```

Press <Enter>.

You can enter a new date in another way as well. Enter the following text, which makes the new date a parameter of the DATE command:

```
DATE 1-1-89<Enter>
```

The computer displays the system prompt. Now when you enter the DATE command again, the computer responds:

```
Current date is Sun 1-01-89
Enter new date:
```

Press <Enter>.

Notice that months and days numbering less than 10 only require one digit. Also, notice that the year doesn't require the century. We just enter 89 or whatever year, and the PC assumes we're in the 1900s.

The PC generates the day of the week through DATE. Enter the following to see what the PC does:

```
DATE 1-1-2000<Enter>
DATE<Enter>
```

The PC should say that the current date is Saturday, January 1, 2000. The computer will accept any date from 1-1-1980 to 12-31-2099. Any dates outside this range will result in:

```
Invalid date
Enter new date:
```

Why a date?   The PC assigns the current system date to any disk data that has been
                    edited, created or modified. This date stamping helps you keep track of
                    the most recent versions of files. The DATE command asks you for
                    today's date.

     Enter the following:

TIME<Enter>

The screen displays this or a similar message:

Current time is: 0:06:00:00
Enter new time:

Enter the current time in HH:MM:SS format. For example, enter the
following to set the time to 10:00 a.m.:

TIME 10:00:00<Enter>

The time setting preceding this change referred to the amount of time
that the PC has been on, if you didn't change it when you started it.
Setting the time when you start the computer is a good habit. Many
computers have built-in battery-powered clocks to keep constant track
of the current time.

You can enter single digits as well. Entering the following for the
time:

TIME 7:5:2<Enter>

Is read by the PC as:

07:05:02

If you enter illegal times like 26:00:00, the PC responds with this or a
similar message:

Invalid time

MS-DOS reads time in 24-hour format. For example, entering the
following sets the time to 5:32 in the evening:

TIME 17:32:00<Enter>

Again, you must remember to press the <Enter> key at the end of
input. This tells the PC to execute the command.

Summary

The DATE and TIME commands let the user set or change the current system date and time at any time. System date and time are stored on disk with any files that are currently updated in any way.

Changing the date requires one of the following entries. The first entry prompts the user for the date, and the second means that the user immediately assigns the date in MM-DD-YY format:

```
DATE<Enter>
DATE MM-DD-YY<Enter>
```

Enter DATE<Enter> alone to display the current date. Press <Enter> to continue.

Changing the time requires one of the following entries. The first entry below prompts the user for the time, and the second immediately assigns the time in HH:MM:SS format:

```
TIME<Enter>
TIME HH:MM:SS<Enter>
```

Enter TIME<Enter> alone to display the current time. Press <Enter> to continue.

2.1.3   The system prompt

You've seen the system prompt (also called the *drive*) many times so far. It indicates the disk drive currently under access, and normally ends with a greater than character. The prompt we've seen so far looks something like this (yours may look different):

A>

You've already read about drive A:. The next disk drive has a *drive specifier* of B:. Hard disks can have drive specifiers of C:, D:, etc. We discussed these drive specifiers briefly in the DISKCOPY command. During the course of this book, we'll refer mainly to drive A: to avoid confusion, since some new PC users actually start out with a single floppy disk drive. We'll discuss other drives (e.g., a hard disk) as the need arises.

Back to the system prompt. The A> simply acts as a visual indicator from the computer to let you know the current cursor location.

You can change the prompt to your own needs. For example, enter the following. Be sure that a space follows the PROMPT command word, or the command won't work:

```
PROMPT I'm waiting for input...<Enter>
```

Now every time the prompt appears, it displays the following instead of A>:

```
I'm waiting for input...
```

Enter the following to get the original prompt back:

```
PROMPT<Enter>
```

The original A> reappears. Enter the following:

```
PROMPT Hello<Enter>
```

Press the <Enter> key several times. Now the PC displays the word Hello, which it wouldn't do for you earlier in this chapter.

The system prompt can serve other purposes. Enter the following and watch the result. Remember to include the space between the command word and the $d characters:

```
PROMPT $D<Enter>
```

The new prompt displays the current system date. You can also have the prompt display the current system time. Enter the following:

```
PROMPT $T<Enter>
```

The system time displayed in the new prompt doesn't change. If you press <Enter> and redisplay the prompt, the time changes.

Enter the following to return the system prompt to normal:

```
PROMPT<Enter>
```

Right now the prompt change is only temporary. In a later chapter we'll show you how to make a new system prompt available permanently. For now you'll have to change the prompt by hand, if you change it at all.

2.1.4   CLS

The CLS command (short for CLear Screen) clears the screen of data. Enter the following to clear the screen:

CLS<Enter>

Summary

PROMPT specifies the appearance of the system prompt, which prompts the PC user for input. The *default* (normal) appearance of the system prompt is as follows on most systems:

A>

Entering the command word PROMPT followed by a space and text changes the A> to the text. For example, this:

PROMPT By your command:

creates a prompt that looks like this:

By your command:

Additional parameters assign different groups of characters to PROMPT. For example, the $D parameter displays the current date, and the $T parameter displays the current time. Entering PROMPT without other parameters returns to the default system prompt A>.

CLS (CLear Screen) clears any text on the screen and displays the system prompt at the upper left corner of the screen.

2.2   Directory display

Let's look at the names of the programs and other data on the system disk. You can't really tell a disk's contents by literally looking at it. However, disks contain listings of their contents called *directories*.

2.2.1   DIR

MS-DOS lets you read directories using the DIR command. If your BACKUP SYSTEM disk isn't in drive A: yet, please insert it now. If your computer and monitor aren't currently turned on, please do so now. Perform whatever tasks you must to get to the system prompt A>.

The DIR command (the abbreviation for DIRectory) displays the directory of the disk as listed in the system prompt.

Enter the following to display the BACKUP SYSTEM disk directory:

DIR<Enter>

The data moves by so quickly that you may not be able to read most of it, at least until the directory stops displaying data. This movement is called *scrolling*, because the information moves past as if you were rolling information past on a scroll.

Your directory may look something like the illustration on the next page. Each program or set of data appears in the listing as follows:

- The leftmost column displays the *filename* (the name of the program/data file).

- The three-letter code following represents the *file extension*, indicating the type of file. .COM and .EXE files are *executable* (running) programs, while .DOC (DOCument) and .TXT (TeXT) files are usually readable text files.

- The numbers represent the size of each file in bytes.

- The last two entries in each line display the date and time that the file was last saved. Notice that all the above files were created or saved on the same date, and that the time uses p to represent p.m. (afternoon).

The end of the directory lists the total number of files and the amount of space remaining on the disk in bytes.

```
Volume in drive A has no label
Directory of  A:\

COMMAND  COM     23210    1-24-86   12:00p
MODE     COM      5386    1-24-86   12:00p
GWBASIC  EXE     70704    1-24-86   12:00p
BASIC    COM       686    1-24-86   12:00p
BASICA   COM       686    1-24-86   12:00p
GRAPHICS COM      6481    1-24-86   12:00p
FORMAT   COM      9390    1-24-86   12:00p
FDISK    COM      5652    1-24-86   12:00p
SYS      COM      3008    1-24-86   12:00p
CHMOD    COM      6704    1-24-86   12:00p
SIZE     COM      4800    1-24-86   12:00p
ASSIGN   COM       864    1-24-86   12:00p
RAMDISK  DEV       768    1-24-86   12:00p
COMP     COM      2845    1-24-86   12:00p
ANSI     SYS      2510    1-24-86   12:00p
PRINT    COM      7043    1-24-86   12:00p
TREE     COM      8955    1-24-86   12:00p
DISKCOMP COM      4074    1-24-86   12:00p
DISKCOPY COM      4665    1-24-86   12:00p
AUTOEXEC BAT         3    1-24-86   12:00p
CHKDSK   COM      9435    1-24-86   12:00p
FIND     EXE      6403    1-24-86   12:00p
README   DOC       256    1-24-86   12:00p
MORE     COM       282    1-24-86   12:00p
        24 File(s)     176000 bytes free
```

2.2.2   Pausing the directory

Reading part of a directory isn't enough—we need to be able to view every filename on the disk. So we need some method of stopping the directory scrolling

Enter the following:

DIR<Enter>

As the directory starts scrolling, press and hold the <Ctrl> key, and briefly press the <S> key. This stops the directory. You should be able to read the first two lines, which look something like this:

```
Volume in drive A: has no label
Directory of A:\
```

Pressing <Ctrl><S> or any letter or number key continues the directory listing.

2.2.3   Stopping commands

There are times when you may want to stop a DOS command as it's running.

Enter the following:

```
DIR<Enter>
```

The directory starts scrolling. Press and hold the <Ctrl> key and press the <C> key. The directory listing stops and the system prompt appears.

Pressing <Ctrl><C> stops most (not all) DOS commands as they execute.

2.2.4   Page display

There's an easier way to display a long directory than <Ctrl><C> or <Ctrl><S>. Make sure that your BACKUP SYSTEM disk is in drive A:. Enter the following:

```
DIR/P<Enter>
```

The /P added to the DIR command tells DOS to display the directory in page format. Watch the display, which will look something like the illustration on the next page.

This page will remain on the screen until you press a key. Once you press a key, the next page of the directory scrolls onto the screen. This continues until the end of the directory.

```
Volume in drive A has no label
Directory of  A:\

COMMAND  COM    23210    1-24-86   12:00p
MODE     COM     5386    1-24-86   12:00p
GWBASIC  EXE    70704    1-24-86   12:00p
BASIC    COM      686    1-24-86   12:00p
BASICA   COM      686    1-24-86   12:00p
GRAPHICS COM     6481    1-24-86   12:00p
FORMAT   COM     9390    1-24-86   12:00p
FDISK    COM     5652    1-24-86   12:00p
SYS      COM     3008    1-24-86   12:00p
CHMOD    COM     6704    1-24-86   12:00p
SIZE     COM     4800    1-24-86   12:00p
ASSIGN   COM      864    1-24-86   12:00p
RAMDISK  DEV      768    1-24-86   12:00p
COMP     COM     2845    1-24-86   12:00p
ANSI     SYS     2510    1-24-86   12:00p
PRINT    COM     7043    1-24-86   12:00p
TREE     COM     8955    1-24-86   12:00p
DISKCOMP COM     4074    1-24-86   12:00p
DISKCOPY COM     4665    1-24-86   12:00p
AUTOEXEC BAT        3    1-24-86   12:00p
CHKDSK   COM     9435    1-24-86   12:00p
FIND     EXE     6403    1-24-86   12:00p
MORE     COM      282    1-24-86   12:00p
Strike a key when ready . . .
```

2.2.5   Changing drive specifiers

Perhaps you have two floppy disk drives. If so, here's your chance to use the second drive. Chapter 1 showed you how to create a backup copy of the DOS system disk using the DISKCOPY command. Now let's make a copy of the other original disk you got with your DOS package. If you didn't get a second disk, just make a backup copy of your BACKUP SYSTEM disk following the instructions below.

Write protect the disk you're about to copy, using either a write protect tab (5-1/4" disks) or opening the write protect slider (3-1/2" disks). Insert the BACKUP SYSTEM disk in drive A: and a blank, unformatted disk in drive B:. Enter the following:

DISKCOPY A: B:<Enter>

When the program finishes loading and asks you to place the source disk in drive A:, remove the BACKUP SYSTEM disk and insert the second original disk. Follow the instructions as stated on the screen. The program tells you when the copy process is complete. When it asks whether you want to copy another disk, press <N> (you may also have to press <Enter>, depending on your DISKCOPY program version).

Enter the following:

B:<Enter>

The system prompt changes from A> to B>. This means that you've assigned disk drive B: as the drive currently being accessed. Any commands you enter are accessed from this drive.

Enter the following:

DIR<Enter>

The directory of drive B: appears on the screen. Enter the following:

A:<Enter>

This changes the system prompt back to A>. Enter the following:

DIR B:<Enter>

Summary

The DIR command displays the current disk directory unless specified otherwise. DIR without other parameters scrolls the directory up the screen without stopping. Pressing <Ctrl><S> pauses the directory display, and pressing any other letter or number key, or even <Ctrl><S>, continues the directory display.

Pressing <Ctrl><C> cancels execution of the DIR command, and many other MS-DOS commands as they execute.

The following command displays the directory in page format (i.e., it waits for a keypress):

DIR/P<Enter>

The directory display begins with a header stating the disk's volume name, if any. Then each file is listed on a line-by-line basis. The file display structure appears as an eight-character filename; a three-character file extension; the file's size in bytes; the creation or most recent date of update. The directory display ends with the number of files currently on the disk, and the number of bytes free.

DOS commands can be redirected to another disk drive by including the drive specifier in the command. For example, the following command entered from drive A: displays the directory of drive B:

```
A>DIR B:<Enter>
```

2.3   Printing from MS-DOS

You may feel that your memory isn't good enough to remember one file out of a directory as it scrolls past. If you have a printer connected to your PC, you can actually send data from the screen to the printer. If you don't own a printer, read this section anyway—you may end up buying one.

2.3.1   Screen hardcopy

If your computer is not connected to the printer, follow your printer's instruction manuals for installation instructions.

<PrtSc>   Turn off the computer and make sure that the printer is connected to the PC, has paper inserted, and is turned on. Insert the DOS disk. Before you turn the PC back on, look on your keyboard for a key marked either <Print> or <PrtSc>, or something similar (we'll call it <PrtSc> in this book). These key names are abbreviations for PRinT SCreen.

When you press and hold a <Shift> key and press the <PrtSc> key, the PC sends a copy of the current screen to the printer, and the printer prints this screen copy. This printout goes under various names— *screen dump*, *screen shot*, *hardcopy*. We'll use the word hardcopy here, since it best defines the transfer from screen to paper (a *hard*, or tangible, medium).

Turn on the PC. Perform whatever tasks you must (if any) to get to the system prompt. When the system prompt appears, press and hold a <Shift> key and press the <PrtSc> key.

The printer starts printing immediately, printing the current contents of the screen on paper.

Problems   If your printer does not respond, check the following:

1. Printer turned on?
2. Printer properly connected to the computer?
3. Printer configuration correct (see printer manual)?
4. If all else fails, call the dealer.

The end result should be a printed copy of the screen.

2.3.2   Directory hardcopy

Now that we've printed a single screen, how can we apply this knowledge to printing something longer, like a disk directory?

If you left the computer on from the last experiment, fine. If not, boot up again and get to the system prompt. Make sure the printer is turned on, connected and fitted with paper.

Press and hold the <Ctrl> key and press the <PrtSc> key. Then enter the following:

```
DIR<Enter>
```

After you press <Enter> the printer proceeds to print the disk directory on paper. Once the printer finishes its job, enter the following:

```
DIR/P<Enter>
```

The printer starts again, and prints one page of the display. Then the following appears on the paper:

```
To continue strike any key . . .
```

Press a key to print the next page. Continue to do this until the printer finishes printing.

You wouldn't normally use DIR/P to print hardcopy, but it's a good demonstration of what <Ctrl><PrtSc> can do. In addition, you can clearly see how many lines of text actually comprise a screen on your computer (usually 25).

Press <Ctrl><PrtSc> to disable the hardcopy process and return output to the screen.

Pressing <Ctrl><S> pauses the printout, which continues if you press the <Enter> key. Pressing <Ctrl><C> stops the printout completely. <Ctrl><PrtSc> disables the printout.

2.3.3   More directory hardcopy

The following prints the directory on paper in a different way. This command sequence actually redirects the output device from the screen to the printer. Enter the following:

```
DIR > PRN<Enter>
```

Unlike <Ctrl><PrtSc>, this redirection becomes inactive after the PC finishes executing the command.

Summary

We printed data from the screen using three methods:

- Pressing the <Shift> key and the <PrtSc> key sends the current contents of the screen to a printer. This process lasts as long as it takes for the screen to print, then returns output to the screen.

- Pressing the <Ctrl> key and the <PrtSc> sends any input from the keyboard and subsequent output to the printer, including commands. This remains active until the user presses <Ctrl><PrtSc> to disable the printed output.

- Redirecting output to a printer for the duration of a command, using the greater than (>) character. Output returns to the screen once the command finishes execution.

2.4   Review

You've learned the following in this chapter:

- The PC's need for an operating system, which it reads from disk.

- The PC only obeys certain commands, and these commands must be entered in a specific way.

- MS-DOS commands can be entered in either upper case or lower case characters.

- The DATE & TIME commands allow you to set the current date and time for accurate time stamping (disk updating).

- The PROMPT command allows you to change the appearance of the system prompt, and even display the current date and time.

- The CLS command clears the screen.

- The DIR command displays the directory of a formatted disk. You can control the scrolling of the directory display by using <Ctrl><S> to stop and start the display.

- Pressing <Ctrl><C> stops the execution of most (not all) MS-DOS commands.

- The DIR/P command displays a disk directory in page format. The PC displays 25 lines of the directory, then prompts the user to press a key to signal the display of the next page.

- The current disk drive can be changed by entering a different drive specifier. For instance, if the current drive is A:, entering B:<Enter> changes the current drive to B:.

- Pressing <Ctrl><PrtSc> sends output currently on the screen to a printer as hardcopy.

- The redirection sequence > PRN sends output to a printer for the duration of a command.

3.

Weekend course in MS-DOS

Now that you've made it through the one-night MS-DOS course, you're ready to take on our weekend program. You don't have to spend an entire weekend doing nothing but studying MS-DOS. If you prefer, you can break the study up into smaller units of time, and spread it over the course of a week. We assumed that you might want to learn as quickly as possible, so we based this chapter on a weekend. Divide your time for this chapter any way you want.

You'll need the following:

- BACKUP SYSTEM disk

- Some blank disks and labels

- A felt-tip pen

3.1 Formatting disks

This section shows you how to format disks, or prepare new disks for accepting data. In Chapter 1 we asked you to buy some new disks so that you could make backup copies of your DOS disks. You should still have a few left over if you bought a set of ten. If not, go buy some more and we'll continue from there. Remember to get quality double-sided, double-density disks.

3.1.1 Why format?

You might be wondering why dealers don't just sell pre-formatted disks. This would take too much effort on the part of disk manufacturers. It's more cost effective for them to sell disks that can be formatted by the user for his or her own purposes.

Insert your BACKUP SYSTEM disk in drive A:. Turn on the monitor and PC and do what you must to get to the system prompt. If your system doesn't ask you for the current date, enter the following:

```
DATE<Enter>
```

When the computer displays its system date, see if that date matches today's date. If it displays today's date, press <Enter>. If not, enter the date following the sample format and press <Enter>.

If your system doesn't ask you for the current time, enter the following:

TIME<Enter>

When the computer displays its system time, see if that time matches the current time. If it displays the current time, press <Enter>. If not, enter the time following the sample format and press <Enter>.

Wait for the system prompt to appear. Take one of the new disks out of the packaging and insert it in drive A:. Close the drive or push the disk into place, depending on your disk drive type. Let's see what's on the disk. Enter the following:

DIR<Enter>

The disk drive runs and the screen displays this or a similar message:

Disk error reading drive A
Abort, Retry, Ignore?

Press the <A> key. Remove this new disk and replace it with the BACKUP SYSTEM disk. The PC cannot use a new, blank disk for data. We must format it.

About FORMAT Think of a newly built, empty warehouse. The owners must plan how they want the warehouse set up for storage: Floor plans must be drawn, shelving built, areas allocated for storing equipment. The FORMAT command works in much the same way. It allocates areas of a disk for storing data in a form readable from a PC.

The FORMAT command is one that must be used with caution, because you can format any disk, old or new. Formatting a disk that already has data on it destroys all the data that once existed.

IBM compatible PCs use the same disk format. This means that if you format a disk, it can be used by any IBM-compatible computer.

3.1.2   Formatting on a single-drive system

Make sure that your BACKUP SYSTEM disk is write protected (see Chapter 1 for write protecting instructions). Insert your BACKUP SYSTEM disk in disk drive A:. Enter the following exactly as it appears (don't press <Enter> when done):

FORMAT A:

Make sure that this is exactly what it says on your screen. Make any corrections if necessary. Now press the <Enter> key. The disk drive runs briefly as it loads the FORMAT command from the BACKUP SYSTEM disk. The screen displays this or a similar message:

```
Insert new disk in drive A:
and press ENTER when ready
```

Transient and resident commands

Some DOS commands are called *resident* because they reside or lie in memory. Resident commands can be accessed immediately (DIR, DATE and TIME are resident commands). Other DOS commands must be loaded in from disk. Since they are kept in memory only for the amount of time they execute, they are known as *transient* commands. FORMAT is a transient command.

Remove the BACKUP SYSTEM disk from drive A:. Take a blank, unformatted disk from your package of new disks and insert this disk in drive A:. Press the <Enter> key. The screen may or may not display a message about its method of formatting a disk. If so, these terms vary with the disk type used. Most 5-1/4" disks have tracks and sectors as mentioned earlier, while many 3-1/2" systems refer to *heads* and *cylinders*. Below the format method stated, the screen displays the progress of the format.

If all goes well, the screen displays the following or a similar message:

```
Formatting completed.
```

Some versions of DOS may ask you to enter a *volume label*. This is just an 11-character disk name, which may come in handy later for disk identification. If a prompt for this appears, just press <Enter> for now.

The screen then displays the following or a similar message:

```
xxx,xxx bytes total disk space
xxx,xxx bytes available on disk
```

The xxx,xxx represents a number—this number varies with the disk type and computer type. The screen then displays this or a similar message:

```
Format another (Y/N)?
```

Enter <Y><Enter> to format another disk. The following or a similar message appears:

```
Insert new disk in drive A:
and press ENTER when ready
```

Remove the newly formatted disk from drive A:. Take a label out of the disk packaging, as you did for labeling the backup disks. Place the label on the disk in a place where it doesn't touch any of the recording media (shiny parts) of the disk. Some manufacturers pre-place labels on their disks for you. If this is the case, just proceed to the next paragraph.

Take the felt-tip pen and write WORK1 on the label. Labeling the disk and writing the name on the label immediately helps avoid confusion. You may only have a few disks now, but as you collect disks, it gets very hard to remember which unlabeled disk is which.

You may not always have a felt-tip pen within reach. If this is the case, place the sheet containing the labels on a table before placing the label on the disk. Write the disk name on the label using a ballpoint pen. Remove the label from the sheet and place it on the disk. **Never write on a labeled disk with ballpoint pen.**

Insert a second unformatted disk in drive A:. Press the <Enter> key to continue. The formatting process begins again. When the formatting procedure ends, the screen displays this or a similar message:

```
Format another (Y/N)?
```

Enter <N><Enter>. The computer exits the FORMAT command and displays a system prompt.

Remove the newly formatted disk from drive A:. If this disk needs labeling, do so now. Take the felt-tip pen and write WORK2 on the label.

Insert the WORK1 disk in drive A:. Enter the following:

```
DIR<Enter>
```

The disk drive runs briefly. The screen displays the following or a similar message:

```
Volume in drive A has no name
Directory of A:\

File not found
```

The system prompt appears. The disk is okay—you just don't have any files on it yet.

Summary   You must format new disks to prepare them for accepting data.

The FORMAT command formats disks.

Resident commands reside in memory for immediate access.

Transient commands must be loaded from a DOS disk.

3.1.3   Formatting on a dual-drive system

Formatting proceeds differently if you own a PC with two floppy disk drives. You can still use the procedure listed in Section 3.1.2, but this method works just as well. Accessing DOS commands with a system disk in drive A: and the disk under access in drive B: offers the advantage of having DOS commands constantly available.

Make sure that your BACKUP SYSTEM disk is write protected (see Chapter 1 for write protecting instructions). Insert your BACKUP SYSTEM disk in disk drive A:. Insert a blank, unformatted disk in drive B: (the drive next to or below drive A:). Enter the following exactly as it appears (don't press <Enter> when done):

FORMAT B:

Make sure that this is exactly what it says on your screen. Make any corrections if necessary. Now press the <Enter> key. The disk drive runs briefly as it loads the FORMAT command from the BACKUP SYSTEM disk. The screen displays this or a similar message:

Insert new disk in drive B:
and press ENTER when ready

Press the <Enter> key. The formatting process begins on drive B:.

You could do this in reverse if you wish. Place the BACKUP SYSTEM disk in drive B: and the disk you want to format in drive A:. Enter the following:

B:<Enter>
FORMAT A:<Enter>

The PC reads the FORMAT command from drive B: and asks you to put the disk you want formatted in drive A:. The process works the same as above.

3.1.4   Formatting on a hard drive system

If your PC came with DOS installed on a hard disk, the process is much the same as if you had two floppy disk drives, with a few small changes.

Reset

Remove any floppy disks from the disk drive. Leave the disk drive lever open. Press and hold the <Ctrl> and <Alt> keys, and press the <Del> key. This action *resets* the computer, which starts the computer from scratch. If DOS is on the hard disk, the computer will go through a sequence similar to that of starting from a floppy disk. Do whatever you must do to get a system prompt. The system prompt should look like this:

C>

Enter the following to get to the main directory of the hard disk:

CD C:\<Enter>

Place the blank disk you want to format into the hard disk. Enter the following exactly as it appears below (don't press the <Enter> key):

FORMAT A:

Make any corrections as needed. Press the <Enter> key and follow the instructions on the screen.

The PC may respond with the following or a similar message:

Bad command or filename

This means your hard disk may not have the FORMAT command available. If not, follow the instructions in Section 3.1.2 for formatting using a single-drive system.

3.2

Creating simple files

We haven't done any really constructive work with DOS. We can enter date and time, read directories, copy disks and format disks. Chapter 1 showed you a little bit about creating a file. We're going to do this again. This section shows you how to create a file and place it in the disk directory.

You may remember that we defined a file as a group of data stored under one name. Each line in a directory listing represents a file. We walked you through creating a simple file named MYFILE.BAT. Let's create another one using the same general procedure.

Make sure that your system prompt reads A> on the screen. Remove the BACKUP SYSTEM disk in drive A: if it's still in the drive. Insert the WORK1 disk in drive A: and enter the following:

```
DIR<Enter>
```

The screen should display:

```
Volume in drive A:  has no label
Directory of a:\
file not found
```

3.2.1   Files are more than typing

Let's leave a memo to your roommate that the computer will display on the screen. If you just enter text, you'll get an error message. Enter the following:

```
Trixie,<Enter>
```

The computer responds with this or a similar message and displays the system prompt:

```
Bad command or file name
```

3.2.2   Writing text with COPY CON

We can't just enter text as you would on a typewriter. The COPY CON command lets us enter data in a file. This isn't the most user-friendly way to create files, but this demonstrates how COPY CON works. Enter the following at the system prompt:

```
COPY CON TRIXIE.TXT<Enter>
```

Here's what you've just done: You told the PC to COPY whatever you enter from the keyboard (the CON device) to a file named TRIXIE.TXT. The COPY command is extremely useful—it copies data from one part of the computer to another. Most often it is used for copying disk files (more on this later), but COPY can also be used for copying files to disk.

CON represents the console device, comprising the screen and keyboard. The word console comes from the early days of computing, when people communicated with large mainframe computers through just a console.

When you press the <Enter> key, the cursor jumps to the next screen line and waits. Enter the following:

```
Trixie,<Enter>
```

Now when you press the <Enter> key, the cursor moves to the next line. Enter the following:

```
I went downtown to the lodge with Ralph.<Enter>
I'll be back before 11 o'clock.<Enter>
Ed<Enter>
```

If you make an error as you enter a line (before pressing <Enter>), use the <Backspace> or <⇐> key to delete the incorrect characters. Enter the correction and press the <Enter> key to move to the next line.

Don't use the arrow keys. You can't move around text in COPY CON as you could with a word processor. Once you press <Enter> you cannot correct the line you just entered.

Make sure that you have pressed <Enter> after the name Ed. Look on the keyboard for the <Ctrl> key at the left side of the keyboard (you used this key earlier to pause the directory display). Press and hold the <Ctrl> key. While you're holding the <Ctrl> key, press and release the <Z> key. Pressing <Ctrl><Z> displays the following on the screen:

```
^Z
```

The ^Z indicates the end of a file. Press the <Enter> key. The disk drive runs. The screen displays the following message:

1 File(s) copied

The system prompt reappears. Enter the following:

DIR<Enter>

The directory lists a file named TRIXIE.TXT as the only file on the disk and displays the system prompt. It also displays the current system time and date, as well as the file's size (under 100 bytes). You now have a file on disk.

3.2.3   Reading text files using TYPE

You can display this file on the screen using the TYPE command. Enter the following to display the file named TRIXIE.TXT:

TYPE TRIXIE.TXT<Enter>

The PC displays the file on the screen, and the system prompt appears after the file ends.

The TYPE command performs the opposite function of COPY CON. Whereas COPY CON copies data from the screen and keyboard to disk, TYPE displays a file's contents on the screen.

Summary   The COPY CON FILENAME sequence copies data entered from the keyboard into a disk file named FILENAME. As with all DOS filenames, the FILENAME parameter can be up to eight characters long, with a three-character file extension.

Errors entered in the current line of a DOS command can be deleted using the <Backspace> or <⇐> key. This key deletes characters to the left of the cursor.

Pressing <Ctrl><Z> indicates the end of a file. Pressing <Enter> after <Ctrl><Z> writes the file to disk.

The DIR command displays this file in the disk directory.

The TYPE FILENAME command sequence displays text files on the screen.

3.2.4   More about COPY CON

Let's explore COPY CON a little further. Enter the following to create a file named TRIAL:

COPY CON TRIAL<Enter>

Now, enter the following text (don't press the <Enter> key):

This is a test. Now is the time for all good men and
women to come to the aid of their party.

Don't press <Enter>. What happened at the right margin? Words may separate at the wrong place when they drop to the next line. COPY CON doesn't offer the flexibility of *word wrap* that you find on word processors.

Continue right where you left off in the text, without pressing <Enter>. Enter the following:

And children. And animals. And other beings.

The PC will probably start beeping round about the words "And other." It won't let you type any characters other than <Enter> at this point. COPY CON allows up to 127 characters in a line. Anywhere past that number, and the computer refuses to let you type any more in the line. Press <Enter> to move to the next line.

Press <Ctrl><Z>, then press the <Enter> key to write the file to the directory.

3.2.5   Exploring filenames

Let's take a closer look at filenames. For a moment, let's pretend that we want to enter a file longer than eight characters. Try entering the following and watch the result:

COPY CON GABRIELLE.TXT<Enter>

The cursor moves to the next line, just as it did when we wrote the memo to Trixie. Enter the following:

Gabrielle,<Enter>
I've gone to the store with Alice.<Enter>
Ralph<Enter>

```
<Ctrl><Z>
<Enter>
```

Enter the following:

```
DIR<Enter>
```

The filename GABRIELL.TXT appears in the directory, but no GABRIELLE.TXT. The PC ignores any characters after the eighth character of a filename. Try entering the following exactly as written notice the placement of spaces):

```
COPY CON MY FILE.TXT<Enter>
```

When you press the <Enter> key, the PC displays this or a similar message:

```
Invalid number of Parameters
```

This means that the PC expected to see only two parameters following the COPY command. The expected parameters were the point of origin of the information (i.e., CON for the console/keyboard) and the destination point of the information (i.e., a filename).

MS-DOS uses spaces to separate many parameters. You cannot use spaces in filenames, since the PC reads the word after the space as another parameter. This is why it displays a message about an invalid number of parameters.

Filenames are limited to certain characters only (see the *filenames* entry in the glossary at the end of this book for more information).

3.2.6   Aborting a file with <Ctrl><C>

Earlier in this book we mentioned that pressing <Ctrl><C> aborts most DOS commands (i.e., stops the command during execution). Enter the following:

```
COPY CON ED.TXT<Enter>
<Enter>
Dear Ed,<Enter>
I'm leaving you for Peter N.<Enter>
Stay out as late as you wish.<Enter>
<Enter>
Trixie<Enter>
```

If you have second thoughts about writing this, press <Ctrl><C> before you press anything else. The system prompt appears. Now if you call a directory with the DIR command, you'll see no file named ED.TXT. You aborted the file by pressing <Ctrl><C>.

Now, enter the CLS command to clear the screen (remember to press <Enter> after entering CLS) and remove any incriminating evidence.

Summary

MS-DOS only accepts filenames which are eight characters in length, with optional three-character extensions. DOS ignores any characters entered beyond the eighth character. (e.g., if you create a file named PHILADELPHIA.TXT, MS-DOS stores the filename as PHILADEL.TXT).

MS-DOS cannot accept spaces within filenames. The PC interprets these as additional parameters.

If you're entering a file using the COPY CON command sequence, you can abort the text entry by pressing <Ctrl><C>.

3.3   Renaming files

This section shows you how to change names in a file. This can be important when you need filenames that clearly state the file's purpose. For example, a file named PETERN12.TXT doesn't tell us much about the contents of the text file, but a file named P_N_XMAS.TXT at least hints that the file is a Christmas letter to someone named P.N.

RENAME

The RENAME command changes the current filename to the specified new filename. Two forms exist of the command: RENAME and REN. Try the long form (RENAME) first. If you get an error message, try the short form (REN)—your version of DOS may not accept one of these versions.

The command syntax for RENAME looks like this (we've included both RENAME and REN here—use whichever syntax works for your version of DOS):

```
RENAME OLD_FILE.EXT NEW_FILE.EXT
REN OLD_FILE.EXT NEW_FILE.EXT
```

Let's look at the file we created for Gabrielle. We entered the name GABRIELLE.TXT, and DOS stored it as GABRIELL.TXT. This name doesn't tell us much. Let's *rename* (change the name of) the file so that we know something of its content.

Make sure the WORK1 disk is in drive A:. Enter the following just to be sure that the file is there:

```
DIR<Enter>
```

The name GABRIELL.TXT should appear somewhere in the directory. Enter the following:

```
RENAME GABRIELL.TXT STORE.TXT<Enter>
```

Some versions of MS-DOS may return an error message about a bad command or filename. If this happens to you, then use the REN command instead:

```
REN GABRIELL.TXT STORE.TXT<Enter>
```

We'll use the word RENAME to describe this command throughout this book. If your system only accepts REN, use this form in place of RENAME when we ask you to enter a command using this word.

The system prompt soon reappears. If you enter the DIR command, you'll see that the file GABRIELL.TXT is gone; it now has the filename STORE.TXT.

Let's make sure that this is the same file. Enter the following:

TYPE STORE.TXT<Enter>

The text appears on the screen:

```
Gabrielle,
I've gone to the store with Alice.
Ralph
```

This very basic text file doesn't look finished somehow. It needs blank lines between paragraphs to make it look more attractive. Since we can't edit a file using COPY CON, let's create a new file instead. Enter the following:

```
COPY CON WOODLAND.TXT<Enter>
<Enter>
<Enter>
<Enter>
<Enter>
<Enter>
<Enter>
<Enter>
<Enter>
<Enter>
Gabrielle,<Enter>
<Enter>
<Enter>
I've gone mall-walking for some exercise.<Enter>
<Enter>
Be back later.<Enter>
<Enter>
Ralph<Enter>
<Ctrl><Z>
<Enter>
```

Here's what you've done: You pressed the <Enter> key ten times to clear some space on the screen. Entering the salutation to Gabrielle, you pressed the <Enter> key three times. Entering your main text, you followed it with two <Enter> keypresses. The closing and the ending name were separated by two <Enter> keypresses. <Ctrl><Z><Enter> closed the file.

Let's see how this looks on the screen. Enter the following:

```
TYPE WOODLAND.TXT<Enter>
```

The text appears on the screen in a better format. The system prompt is too close to the name Ralph; we could have added a few blank lines before the <Ctrl><Z>.

Now, let's change the filename to something more meaningful. Maybe WOODLAND is the name of a shopping mall; we don't know that. Changing the name to a more clearly understood name helps anyone to follow what the file is about. Enter the following (use REN instead of RENAME if your system prefers that command word):

```
RENAME WOODLAND.TXT MALLWALK.TXT<Enter>
```

The file remains the same—only the name has been changed.

We mentioned earlier that we didn't include enough space between the last line of text and the end of the file. Let's experiment with that. Enter the following:

```
COPY CON MILLER.TXT<Enter>
<Enter>
<Enter>
<Enter>
Dear Ralph,<Enter>
<Enter>
<Enter>
I've gone to the Millers' apartment.<Enter>
<Enter>
We're going to the Million Screen Theatre.<Enter>
<Enter>
Please meet us there for the 9:30 show!<Enter>
<Enter>
<Enter>
Alice<Enter>
<Enter>
<Enter>
<Enter>
```

<Ctrl><Z>
<Enter>

Enter the following to see the text:

TYPE MILLER.TXT<Enter>

Maybe you're still not satisfied. Enter the following:

COPY CON MILLER.TXT<Enter>

If you continue, this action overwrites the file you just created. Data will be stored in a new file named MILLER.TXT. Be careful when using COPY CON, and make sure that a filename doesn't already exist before using it. For now, enter the following to exit COPY CON without overwriting the MILLER.TXT file:

<Ctrl><C>

A problem arises if you try renaming a file to an existing name. Enter the following and watch the result:

RENAME MILLER.TXT STORE.TXT<Enter>

This or a similar message appears on the screen:

Duplicate filename or File not found

This keeps you from accidentally destroying the other file.

Summary

We can rename files using the RENAME command (called REN in some systems). The syntax of RENAME appears in these forms:

RENAME OLDFILE.EXT NEWFILE.EXT
REN OLDFILE.EXT NEWFILE.EXT

If a file already exists on disk with a name matching the NEWFILE.EXT parameter, the PC responds with an error message.

3.4   Copying output to a printer

Chapter 2 showed you how to redirect the directory output to a printer. We can also send file output to a printer.

Make sure that you still have the WORK1 disk in drive A: with the files that you created in Section 3.3. Make sure that the printer is connected to the correct port on your PC, has paper in it, and is switched on. Enter the following:

CLS<Enter>

Press <Ctrl><PrtSc>. Nothing happens at first. Any subsequent output will go to the printer. You should still have the MALLWALK.TXT file on disk. Enter the following to print it out:

TYPE MALLWALK.TXT<Enter>

This file appears both on the screen and on the printer. Unfortunately, <Ctrl><PrtSc> sends everything else on the screen to the printer, including the command you just entered. This is fine for a rough draft, but it doesn't look very good in a final printout. Press <Ctrl><PrtSc> again to disable the screen hardcopy command.

Let's use COPY CON to send a text file to the printer. Enter the following:

COPY CON PRN<Enter>

The cursor moves to the next line. Nothing happens on the printer (this is fine—be patient). Enter the following text, which is a thank-you note to someone's aunt for a gift:

Dear Aunt Annie,<Enter>
<Enter>
Thank you very much for the birthday present. I hope that
you and<Enter>
Uncle Clem will be able to visit this weekend. I'll call
you on<Enter>
Thursday to confirm.<Enter>
<Enter>
Love,<Enter>
<Enter>
Dick<Enter>

```
<Ctrl><Z>
<Enter>
```

When you press <Ctrl><Z> and <Enter>, this letter goes to the printer. After the printer finishes printing the text, the end of text marker (^Z) automatically returns MS-DOS to normal screen display.

Now let's take an existing text file and print it. Enter the following:

```
COPY MALLWALK.TXT PRN<Enter>
```

When you press <Enter>, the PC prints the MALLWALK.TXT file on the printer. Each filename you created using COPY CON can be copied to the printer. Try each one of these:

```
COPY STORE.TXT PRN<Enter>
```

```
COPY TRIAL PRN<Enter>
```

```
COPY MILLER.TXT PRN<Enter>
```

You'll soon see that COPY has many more capabilities—more on this in the next section.

Summary   COPY CON FILENAME allows you to create simple text files.

Pressing <Ctrl><Z> and <Enter> closes a file opened by COPY CON filename.

Pressing <Ctrl><C> aborts text input to a file created using COPY CON.

COPY CON PRN lets you send text direct from the console (keyboard and screen) to the printer. Printing begins when you press <Ctrl><Z><Enter> to indicate the end of the file.

COPY CON FILENAME PRN sends a text file to a connecting, active printer instead of the screen. This form of printing is much neater than pressing <Ctrl><PrtSc>, which prints everything on the screen.

3.5   Copying files

The WORK1 disk should contain the files `STORE.TXT`, `MALLWALK.TXT`, `TRIAL`, `MILLER.TXT` and `TRIXIE.TXT`. Make sure this disk is inserted in drive A:.

Imagine that you want to transfer one of these files to another disk.

3.5.1   Why copy?

Why make copies? You might have a text file you want to pass along to a friend. Or you might want to create a backup of a file on another disk, in case the original file is destroyed. It doesn't take much to damage a disk. Tobacco ashes, coffee, Szechuan sauce and magnets are potential hazards to disks.

Let's create a reading list file. This reading list contains books that would be of interest if you were preparing to go to Rome. Enter the following:

```
COPY CON ROMELIST.TXT<Enter>
```

The filename `ROMELIST.TXT` describes a list of books about Rome. Remember that the PC only accepts filenames of eight characters or less, and three-character file extensions.

Enter the following names. Only press <Enter> when we tell you to press <Enter>, since some of these names wrap around in this text:

```
J. E. Fisher, Rome: Enjoying It More (J.R.R. Pub.)<Enter>
- , Yet Another Melting Pot—Rome<Enter>
J. W. Schentzow, Knowing and Loving Rome (Random Access
House)<Enter>
<Ctrl><Z>
<Enter>
```

Use the `DIR` command to make sure the `ROMELIST.TXT` file is on the disk.

Your friend Herb stops by. You print your file for him. He's going to Rome in a month, and would like his own disk copy of the file. You can make a copy of this file for him on disk.

Back in Chapter 1 we used the DISKCOPY command to duplicate entire disks. Let's review the procedure, looking at different methods of using DISKCOPY, and copy the WORK1 disk to make a duplicate for Herb. Use whichever procedure suits your system.

You will need:

- The WORK1 disk, containing the ROMELIST.TXT file

- A blank disk

3.5.2   DISKCOPY—dual-drive systems

Make sure that the disk you want to copy is write protected using a write protect tab or sliding the write protect notch, depending on your disk format. Insert the BACKUP SYSTEM disk in drive A:. Make sure that the system prompt reads as follows:

```
A>
```

Enter the following:

```
DISKCOPY A: B:<Enter>
```

MS-DOS displays the following or a similar line:

```
Insert source diskette in Drive A:
Insert target diskette in Drive B:
Press any key when ready...
```

Remove the BACKUP SYSTEM disk from drive A:. Insert the write protected disk you want to copy (WORK1) in drive A:. Insert a blank disk in drive B:. Press the key your system asks you to press. The following or similar messages appear (the numbers change depending on the disk format):

```
Copying 40 (80) tracks
9 Sectors/Track, 2 Side(s)

Formatting diskette during copying
```

After some time the following or a similar message appears:

```
Copy complete
Copy another diskette (Y/N)?
```

Press the <N> key and wait a moment. If the PC doesn't respond, press the <Enter> key and wait until the system prompt reappears. Remove the new copy from drive B: and label immediately as WORK3.

3.5.3

DISKCOPY—single-drive systems

Make sure that the disk you want to copy is write protected using a write protect tab or sliding the write protect notch, depending on your disk format. Insert the BACKUP SYSTEM disk in drive A:. Make sure that the system prompt reads as follows:

```
A>
```

Enter the following:

```
DISKCOPY A: A:<Enter>
```

MS-DOS displays the following or a similar line:

```
Insert source diskette in Drive A:
Press any key when ready...
```

Remove the BACKUP SYSTEM disk from drive A:. Insert the write protected disk you want to copy in drive A:. Press the key your system asks you to press. The following or similar messages appear (the numbers change depending on the disk format):

```
Copying 40 (80) tracks
9 Sectors/Track, 2 Side(s)

Insert target diskette in Drive A:
Press any key when ready...
```

Remove the source disk from drive A:. Insert a blank disk in drive A:. Press the key your system asks you to press. The following or a similar message appears:

```
Formatting diskette during copying
```

After some time the following or a similar message appears:

```
Copy complete
Copy another diskette (Y/N)?
```

Press the <N> key and wait a moment. If the PC doesn't respond, press the <Enter> key and wait until the system prompt reappears. Remove the disk from drive A: and label it immediately as WORK3.

3.5.4   DISKCOPY—hard drive systems

If your DOS commands are available on your hard disk, you should be able to access DISKCOPY from there. Insert the write protected source disk in the disk drive. Make sure the system prompt looks like this:

C>

If not, enter the following:

C:<Enter>

Enter the following:

DISKCOPY A: A:<Enter>

MS-DOS displays the following or a similar message:

```
Insert source diskette in Drive A:
Press any key when ready...
```

Press the key your system asks you to press. The following or similar messages appear (the numbers change depending on the disk format):

```
Copying 40 (80) tracks
9 Sectors/Track, 2 Side(s)

Insert target diskette in Drive A:
Press any key when ready...
```

Remove the source disk from drive A:. Insert a blank disk in drive A:. Press the key your system asks you to press. The following or a similar message appears:

```
Formatting diskette during copying
```

After some time the following or a similar message appears:

```
Copy complete
Copy another diskette (Y/N)?
```

Press the <N> key and wait a moment. If the PC doesn't respond, press the <Enter> key and wait until the system prompt reappears. Remove the disk from drive A: immediately and label it as WORK3.

3.6　　The COPY command

`DISKCOPY` is fine for copying entire disks, but suppose you have a disk that contains information you don't want copied (e.g., with text files to your roommate)? We need a command for copying individual files.

You've already used the `COPY` command for creating files from the console, and for sending existing text to a printer. However, the `COPY` command has one major purpose: Copying one or more files. There are three ways of copying files, depending on your disk drive configuration. Use whichever procedure matches your system.

You will need:

- The WORK1 disk with the file `ROMELIST.TXT`

- The WORK2 disk

- Write protect tab (5-1/4" disks only)

3.6.1　　`COPY`—dual-drive systems

Write protect the WORK1 disk and place it in disk drive A:. Insert the disk labeled WORK2 in drive B:. Make sure that the system prompt reads A>.

Enter the following (notice the placement of spaces):

```
COPY ROMELIST.TXT B:<Enter>
```

Drive A: runs for a moment, then drive B:. Next the screen displays this or a similar message:

```
1 file(s) copied.
```

Enter the following:

```
B:<Enter>
DIR <Enter>
```

The directory listing for drive B: displays the filename `ROMELIST.TXT`. Go on to Section 3.6.4.

3.6.2   COPY—single-drive systems

Write protect the WORK1 disk and place it in disk drive A:. Make sure that the system prompt reads A>.

Enter the following (notice the placement of spaces):

```
COPY ROMELIST.TXT B:<Enter>
```

Even though you don't have a drive B:, this command tells the PC to treat drive A: as a virtual drive B:. Virtual means that the drive doesn't really exist, but that the PC uses drive A: as a pseudo drive B:.

Drive A: runs for a moment. The screen displays this or a similar message:

```
Insert diskette for drive B:
Press any key when ready ...
```

Remove the WORK1 disk from drive A:. Insert the disk labeled WORK2 in drive A: and press a key. Drive A: runs for a moment and the screen displays this or a similar message:

```
1 file(s) copied
```

The screen may also display this or a similar message. If so, do as it says and insert the WORK1 disk in drive A: again:

```
Insert diskette for drive A:
Press any key when ready ...
```

Press a key and wait until the system prompt reappears. Remove the WORK1 disk from drive A: and insert the WORK2 disk in drive A:. Enter the following:

```
DIR <Enter>
```

The directory listing for drive A: displays the filename ROMELIST.TXT.

Go on to Section 3.6.4.

3.6.3   COPY—hard drive systems

We own a PC with one drive and a hard disk drive. To copy individual files we must proceed as follows:

Insert the WORK1 disk containing the ROMELIST.TXT file in drive A:. Make sure the system prompt reads A>. Enter one of the following:

```
COPY ROMELIST.TXT C:<Enter>
COPY A:ROMELIST.TXT C:<Enter>
```

This copies the file to the hard disk drive.

Remove the WORK1 disk from drive A: and insert the WORK2 disk in drive A:. Enter the following to change the current drive to the hard disk drive:

```
C:<Enter>
```

Enter one of the following:

```
COPY ROMELIST.TXT A:<Enter>
COPY C:ROMELIST.TXT A:<Enter>
```

This copies the file from the hard disk to the WORK2 disk in drive A:. When the system prompt reappears, remove the WORK2 disk from drive A:.

You must remove the ROMELIST.TXT file from the hard disk using the DEL command. We'll discuss this command in detail in Section 3.8 below. For now, however, enter the following:

```
DEL C:ROMELIST.TXT<Enter>
```

As you become more proficient in MS-DOS, you'll use your hard disk more and more to store files, using floppy disks for transfer and backup only.

3.6.4   Copying files within a disk

You can copy files on a disk, provided that you assign the target filename a different name from the original file.

Insert the WORK1 disk in drive A: and enter the following:

```
COPY CON LETTER.TXT<Enter>
<Enter>
Alice,<Enter>
<Enter>
I'll be back in a minute.<Enter>
<Enter>
Ralph<Enter>
<Ctrl><Z>
<Enter>
```

Now we have a file named LETTER.TXT on this disk. Our task now is to duplicate this file.

Enter the following, and watch the result:

```
COPY LETTER.TXT<Enter>
```

The PC displays an error message:

```
File cannot be copied onto itself
```

We cannot make duplicate files of the same name. However, we can copy the file to other files with similar names. Enter the following:

```
COPY LETTER.TXT NEWLETT.TXT<Enter>
```

The disk drive runs for a moment. The following message appears on the screen:

```
1 File(s) copied
```

If you enter a DIR command you'll see files named LETTER.TXT and NEWLETT.TXT. Enter the following DOS commands to create three more copies of the same file on disk (you'll need these for Chapter 4):

```
COPY LETTER.TXT LETTER1.TXT<Enter>
COPY LETTER.TXT LETTER2.TXT<Enter>
COPY LETTER.TXT LETTER3.TXT<Enter>
```

3.6.5   Copying files to other disks (new names)

You can also copy one file to other disks and assign the target files new names. Each procedure is listed below.

Double drives: Place the WORK1 disk in drive A: and the WORK2 disk in drive B:. Enter the following:

```
COPY A:LETTER.TXT B:NEWFILE.TXT<Enter>
```

This copies the file to drive B: under the name NEWFILE.TXT. Go on to the Summary.

Single drive: Insert the WORK1 disk in drive A:. Since you have no drive B:, the COPY command will have to treat drive A: as a virtual disk drive. Enter the following:

```
COPY A:LETTER.TXT B:NEWFILE.TXT<Enter>
```

Follow the instructions on the screen and insert the WORK2 disk when the system asks for the drive B: disk. Go on to the Summary below.

Hard drives: Insert the WORK1 disk in drive A:. Enter the following:

```
COPY A:LETTER.TXT C:NEWFILE.TXT<Enter>
```

Remove the WORK1 disk from drive A: and insert the WORK2 disk in drive A:. Enter the following:

```
COPY C:NEWFILE.TXT A:<Enter>
```

This copies the file to drive A: under the name NEWFILE.TXT.

Summary

MS-DOS provides two ways of copying individual files:

1.   Copying files from one disk to another. The following copies the file FILENAME from drive A: to drive B, retaining the filename used on drive A:

      COPY FILENAME B:
      COPY A:FILENAME B:

      Single-drive system owners must change disks when the computer requests the change. Hard disk system owners should use the hard disk as temporary storage.

2.   Copying files to the same disk with different filenames. The following copies the file OLDNAME to the same disk under the name NEWNAME:

      COPY OLDNAME NEWNAME

      If the NEWNAME matches an existing file, the existing file will be overwritten by the copied file.

3.   Copying a file to another disk under a new name:

      COPY LETTER.TXT B:NEWLETT.TXT
      COPY A:LETTER.TXT B:NEWLETT.TXT

      If the NEWNAME matches an existing file, the existing file will be overwritten by the copied file.

      Single-drive system owners must change disks when the computer requests the change. Hard disk system owners should use the hard disk as temporary storage.

3.7   Naming disks

We mentioned earlier that as you collect disks, you'll find it harder and harder to keep track of them. MS-DOS offers ways to keep disks orderly.

You will need the following for this section:

- The WORK1, WORK2 and WORK3 disks, as well as your BACKUP SYSTEM disk

- Blank disks

- Labels

- felt-tip pen

Let's take a prime example—the WORK1 disk which we've been using for most of our experiments so far. Enter the DIR command (remember to press the <Enter> key), and the display will look something like this:

```
Volume in drive A: has no label
Directory of A:\

STORE       TXT           93    3-09-89    2:40p
TRIAL                    129    3-09-89    2:43p
TRIXIE      TXT           64    3-09-89    2:46p
MILLER      TXT          162    3-09-89    6:21p
MALLWALK    TXT          114    3-09-89    6:20p
ROMELIST    TXT          140    3-09-89    9:11a
LETTER      TXT          143    3-09-89    9:19a
NEWLETT     TXT          143    3-09-89    9:19a
LETTER1     TXT          143    3-09-89    9:19a
LETTER2     TXT          143    3-09-89    9:19a
LETTER3     TXT          143    3-09-89    9:19a
        11 file(s)    351232 bytes free
```

This may be slightly different from your own directory. No matter.

Notice the first line:

```
Volume in drive A: has no label
```

LABEL

We can actually insert a name in this line, which will help avoid confusion. The LABEL command performs this task.

The following is a generic procedure that can be used by any system (single-drive, dual-drive, hard disk). For those of you dual-drive users who want another way out, read on.

Since LABEL is a transient command (i.e., it must be loaded from disk), we must start with a DOS disk in the current disk drive. Remove the WORK1 disk from drive A: and replace it with your BACKUP SYSTEM disk. Enter the following:

```
LABEL A:<Enter>
```

The disk drive runs for a moment and this or a similar message appears on the screen:

```
Volume in drive A: has no label
Volume label (max. 11 characters) or ENTER for none?
```

Don't touch any keys. Remove the BACKUP SYSTEM disk from drive A: and replace it with your WORK1 disk. Enter the name WORK1 and press the <Enter> key. The disk drive runs briefly. When you invoke the DIR command, the first line of the directory listing looks like this:

```
Volume in drive A: is WORK1
Directory of A:\
```

Seeing this volume label can be especially important in helping you tell one printed directory listing from another.

Dual drives:

This use of LABEL can be used by any disk configuration (single drive, dual-drives or hard disk). However, dual-drive system users can use an alternate syntax of the LABEL command.

Insert the BACKUP SYSTEM disk in drive A:, and the WORK1 disk in drive B:. Enter the following:

```
LABEL B:<Enter>
```

When the prompt appears as above, enter WORK1 and press the <Enter> key. Enter the following to check the volume name:

```
DIR B:<Enter>
```

Assign volume labels to the WORK2 and WORK3 disks using the procedures for LABEL.

You remember that we copied some files to the disk WORK2. Insert WORK2 in drive A: and enter:

```
DIR A:<Enter>
```

It contains the following files:

```
Volume in drive A: is WORK2
Directory of A:\

ROMELIST     TXT          140   10-25-87     9:11a
NEWFILE      TXT          143   10-25-87     9:19a
LETTER3      TXT          143   10-25-87     9:19a
          2 file(s)     360448 bytes free
```

Finally we still have WORK3 which was created with DISKCOPY from WORK1, but does not contain all the same files because some were created after DISKCOPY. Remove WORK2 from drive A: and insert the WORK3 disk in drive A:. Enter the following:

```
DIR A:<Enter>
```

The directory listing looks something like this:

```
Volume in drive A: is WORK3
Directory of A:\

LETTER3      TXT          143   10-25-87     9:19a
STORE        TXT           93   10-23-87     2:40p
TRIAL                     129   10-23-87     2:43p
GABRIELL     TXT           64   10-23-87     2:46p
MILLER       TXT          162   10-24-87     6:21p
MALLWALK     TXT          114   10-24-87     6:20p
ROMELIST     TXT          140   10-25-87     9:11a
          6 file(s)     356352 bytes free
```

VOL

The first line of the directory listing describes something called a *volume*. The disk names WORK1, WORK2 and WORK3 are volume labels. Using the VOL command, we can read volume names without listing the entire directory. Insert the WORK1 disk in drive A: and enter one of the following:

VOL<Enter>
VOL A:<Enter>

The following or a similar message appears:

Volume in drive A: is WORK1

VOL lets you read the volume name of the disk currently in the drive at any time. VOL is a resident command (i.e., it resides in memory and doesn't have to be read from disk).

Options

You can assign volume names as you format disks as well. Many DOS commands have extra parameters called *options*. These options turn certain command options on or off, depending on whether the option is normally active or inactive. Options appear as slash characters followed by a number or letter (e.g., /V or /S).

Let's format another disk. This time, however, we'll add an option to the FORMAT command that instructs MS-DOS to prompt us for a volume name. Insert your BACKUP SYSTEM disk in drive A:. Enter the following (be absolutely sure to include the slash character and the letter V):

FORMAT A:/V<Enter>

The /V stands for Volume. When DOS prompts you to insert the disk you want formatted, remove the BACKUP SYSTEM disk and insert a blank disk. Press the key your system asks you to press.

While the disk is formatting, take your labels and a felt-tip pen. Write WORK4 on one of the labels.

After the formatting procedure ends, the screen displays this or a similar message:

Volume label (max. 11 characters) or ENTER for none?

Enter:

WORK4<Enter>

Remove the WORK4 label from the sheet and place it on the disk, away from any magnetic media openings.

Dual drives: If you have two floppy disk drives, you can perform this same task with the BACKUP SYSTEM disk in drive A: and the disk you want to format in drive B:. Enter the following:

```
FORMAT B:/V<Enter>
```

Follow the instructions on the screen as indicated for the single drive instructions.

CHKDSK   MS-DOS offers another command for checking disks. The CHKDSK command (short for CHecKDiSK) looks at the memory usage and file status of the disk and of your PC's memory usage. CHKDSK is a transient command, and therefore must be loaded from disk.

Different ways exist for using CHKDSK on different disk systems. To demonstrate this, you'll need your BACKUP SYSTEM disk and the WORK1 disk for all the instructions below.

Single-drive and hard disk systems: Make sure that your system prompt reads A>. Remove any disk that might be in drive A: and insert your BACKUP SYSTEM disk in drive A:. Enter the following:

```
CHKDSK B:<Enter>
```

The PC loads the command and displays this or a similar message:

```
Insert diskette for drive B:
and press Enter when ready ...
```

Remove the BACKUP SYSTEM disk from drive A: and insert the WORK1 disk in drive A:. Press the key your system tells you to press.

Dual-drive: Make sure that your system prompt reads A>. Remove any disk that might be in drive A:. Insert your BACKUP SYSTEM disk in drive A: and your WORK1 disk in drive B:. Enter the following:

```
CHKDSK B:<Enter>
```

Watch the screen.

Hard disks: To check the hard disk, place your BACKUP SYSTEM disk in drive A:. Enter the following:

```
CHKDSK C:<Enter>
```

Your screen will look something like this (numbers vary because of system date, time and memory configuration):

```
Volume WORK1
created Oct 25, 1987 10.33a

   362496 bytes total disk space
        0 bytes in 1 hidden files
    11264 bytes in 11 user files
   351232 bytes available on disk

   655360 bytes total memory
   607520 bytes free
```

The CHKDSK command checks the amount of memory occupied by files on the disk; the types of files stored (user or *hidden*), and errors found on the disk. The end of the CHKDSK display tells you how much total memory your PC has, and how much of this memory is currently available to you.

When errors occur during formatting, CHKDSK tells you about these errors and asks if you want DOS to try repairing the errors.

Summary

Assigning names to disks helps you keep organized, using the following procedures:

- Clearly label your disks immediately after formatting them, using the labels provided with your disks.

- Assign volume names to your disks when formatting. Using the FORMAT /V command formats a blank disk and prompts you for a volume name.

- Already formatted disks can also be assigned volume names. The LABEL command prompts you for a volume name.

- Volume names can be read at any time by entering the VOL command.

The CHKDSK command displays the current disk status, the number of files on the disk, errors on the disk, total memory available on your PC and free memory currently available to you.

3.8   Deleting files

This section shows you in detail how to *delete* (remove) existing files from disk. Insert your WORK2 disk in drive A: and enter the following:

DIR<Enter>

The WORK2 directory displays the files ROMELIST.TXT, NEWFILE.TXT and LETTER3.TXT. Remember that NEWFILE.TXT is a copy of LETTER.TXT, as is LETTER3.TXT.

DEL
ERASE

We should delete the unnecessary file to keep things organized. MS-DOS has a command specifically created for deleting files. This command has two names, ERASE or DEL (short for DELete).

> **DEL**   Make sure the WORK2 disk is in drive A:. Enter the following:
>
> COPY CON SCRAP.TXT<Enter>
> TEXT<Enter>
> <Ctrl><Z>
> <Enter>
>
> This creates a file on the disk named SCRAP.TXT. Enter the following to see the DEL command works:
>
> DEL SCRAP.TXT<Enter>
>
> **ERASE**   The ERASE command works exactly like the DEL command:
>
> ERASE SCRAP.TXT<Enter>

DIR

Check the directory of the WORK2 disk with DIR. You'll see that the file SCRAP.TXT no longer exists.

Use DEL with caution! One feature of DIR allows you to search for individual files in a directory. It's too easy to enter DEL FILENAME.EXT instead of DIR FILENAME.EXT, and accidentally delete the file you wanted to find.

Let's get some deleting practice in. Enter the following to create a file:

```
COPY CON SCRAP.TXT<Enter>
TEXT<Enter>
<Ctrl><Z>
<Enter>
```

Now that you've created this file, enter the following to make copies of the file on the WORK2 disk:

```
COPY SCRAP.TXT SCRAP1.TXT<Enter>
COPY SCRAP.TXT SCRAP2.TXT<Enter>
```

Use the DIR command to make sure these files exist on disk. Now you can start deleting some of these files. Enter the following (remember to use your system's version of DEL):

```
DEL SCRAP.TXT<Enter>
DEL SCRAP1.TXT<Enter>
DEL SCRAP2.TXT<Enter>
```

Use the DIR command to ensure that these files are now gone.

3.9   Review

Let's review what we've learned so far:

- The DISKCOPY command makes duplicates of entire disks. We used this command to make backup copies of our DOS disks.

- The DATE and TIME commands assign the date and time entered by the user as the current system date and time.

- The PROMPT command lets the user change the appearance of the system prompt.

- The CLS command clears the screen of data and places the system prompt at the upper left corner of the screen.

- The DIR command displays the current disk directory. The DIR/P command displays the disk directory in page format (i.e., 23 lines of directory text, then a prompt to press a key to see the next page).

- Printed copies of the screen can be produced in a number of ways: Pressing <PrtSc> to create a screen hardcopy; pressing <Ctrl><PrtSc> to print command execution; and redirecting output using the > character. Entering DIR > PRN prints the directory straight to a printer. The > redirection becomes inactive after the command finishes execution.

- The FORMAT command formats disks for accepting MS-DOS data.

- MS-DOS has two types of commands: resident (directly accessible from memory) and transient (must be loaded from disk). DIR is resident, while FORMAT is transient.

- The COPY CON command sequence takes data entered at the keyboard and sends this data to a disk file when the user ends input by pressing <Ctrl><Z> and <Enter>.

- MS-DOS only accepts filenames up to eight characters long. If spaces are inserted in a filename, MS-DOS will not accept the filename.

- The RENAME command changes an existing filename to a new filename specified by the user.

- The DISKCOPY command can be used on single-drive systems (using DISKCOPY A: A:), dual-drive systems (DISKCOPY A: B:) and hard drive systems (DISKCOPY A: A:).

- The COPY command lets the user copy individual files from one disk to another (e.g., COPY A:FILENAME B:). The user can also copy files to the same or another disk under a different filename (e.g., COPY A:OLDNAME B:NEWNAME, COPY A:OLDNAME NEWNAME).

- The LABEL command allows the user to assign volume names to disks, to help keep disks organized.

- Formatting disks using the /V option prompts the user for a volume name as a disk is formatting (e.g., FORMAT A:/V).

- The VOL command lets the user view the volume name of a disk at any time.

- The DEL command deletes the specified file from the directory (e.g., DEL FILENAME).

4.   MS-DOS   shortcuts

Now that you've learned something about the most basic MS-DOS commands, we'd like to share some tricks and tips with you to help make your sessions with MS-DOS easier and more productive.

For this chapter you'll need:

•   Your BACKUP SYSTEM disk

•   The WORK1, WORK2, WORK3 and WORK4 disks

4.1   Wildcards

A wildcard acts in much the same way as a wildcard used in card games. MS-DOS wildcards can replace one or more characters. These wildcards are often used in copying and deleting multiple files.

You saw in Chapter 3 the importance of being able to copy and delete files. Your WORK1 disk should contain a number of files you generated in Chapter 3, including `NEWLETT.TXT`, `LETTER1.TXT`, `LETTER2.TXT` and `LETTER3.TXT`. These four files are identical in content and size—only the filenames differ from one another.

Create a fourth slightly different file by entering the following:

```
COPY CON LETTER4.TXT<Enter>
Dear Harold,<Enter>
<Ctrl><Z>
<Enter>
```

4.1.1   The asterisk

Now, suppose you needed to copy all the files starting with the filename `LETTER` to another disk (e.g., `LETTER.TXT`, `LETTER1.TXT`, `LETTER2.TXT`, etc.). The most obvious procedure would be to copy each file to another disk one at a time (don't do anything yet, just read on):

```
COPY A:LETTER.TXT B:
COPY A:LETTER1.TXT B:
COPY A:LETTER2.TXT B:
COPY A:LETTER3.TXT B:
```

There's an easier way. The *asterisk* wildcard replaces groups of characters. This lets us perform multiple file copying with just one command line.

Insert your WORK1 disk in drive A:. If you have a second drive, insert your WORK2 disk in drive B:—if you only have one drive, keep the WORK2 disk handy anyway. Enter the following:

```
COPY A:LETTER*.TXT B:<Enter>
```

This copies all the .TXT files whose names begin with LETTER over to drive B:. If you have a single disk drive, follow the instructions on the screen for exchanging disks. When the procedure ends, the following appears on the screen:

```
6 File(s) copied
```

Asterisks can also replace file extensions. For example, the following command copies all filenames starting with T, including any file extensions, to drive B:

```
COPY A:T*.* B:
```

4.1.2 Renaming files using asterisks

The asterisk wildcard works with the RENAME command as well as the COPY command. Almost every file you've entered so far has had a file extension. You'll now see how to add extensions to extensionless files using asterisks and the RENAME command.

Insert the WORK1 disk into drive A:. Enter the following (remember— do <u>not</u> enter a period or a file extension):

```
COPY CON NOEXTEN1<Enter>
Text<Enter>
<Ctrl><Z>
<Enter>
```

Now enter the following to make copies of this file:

```
COPY NOEXTEN1 NOEXTEN2<Enter>
COPY NOEXTEN1 NOEXTEN3<Enter>
COPY NOEXTEN1 NOEXTEN4<Enter>
COPY NOEXTEN1 NOEXTEN5<Enter>
COPY NOEXTEN1 NOEXTEN6<Enter>
```

Now enter the following to add `.TXT` entensions to all these files (remember to include a space between the `NOEXTEN*` filename and the `NOEXTEN*.TXT` filename):

```
RENAME NOEXTEN* NOEXTEN*.TXT<Enter>
```

Invoke a directory with `DIR`, and you'll see the changed filenames.

Now, let's rename the `LETTER` files so that they have extensions of `.BAK` (short for BAcKup). Enter the following:

```
RENAME LETTER*.TXT LETTER*.BAK<Enter>
```

Invoke a directory using the `DIR` command to see the result.

Here are a list of file extensions that you should be very careful not to confuse. One typing error could destroy some very important data. This list contains the most frequently seen extensions, but the list is by no means complete:

BAK   Backup copy of a file

BAS   Program in the computer language BASIC

BAT   Batch file (more on these in Chapter 6)

COM   Command (program) file

EXE   Executable (program) file

DOC   Document file, usually used with Microsoft Word

TXT   Text files, normally used in word processing

4.1.3   Deleting all files using asterisks

Using the `DEL` command in conjunction with asterisk wildcards can delete multiple files on a disk. However, you could delete files you don't want deleted if you don't proceed with caution.

Make sure that the system prompt reads A>. Pick up the WORK2 disk but **do not** insert the WORK2 disk in drive A:. Enter the following (don't press the <Enter> key yet):

```
DEL A:*.*
```

WAIT! Before inserting the disk and pressing the <Enter> key, think of what you're about to do. The asterisks replace any combination of letters and numbers. This means that if you press the <Enter> key with a disk in the drive, DEL A:*.* deletes **everything** on the disk in drive A:.

Ask yourself if you really want to delete all the files on the disk. Is this the correct disk? In this case, we want you to delete the files off of the WORK2 disk, since it only contains duplicates of existing files. Insert the WORK2 disk in drive A: and press the <Enter> key. The PC displays the following or a similar message on the screen:

```
Are you sure? (Y/N)
```

Press <Y><Enter>. The drive runs for a moment. If you invoke a DIR command, the directory responds with the message:

```
File not found
```

The original versions of these files were on WORK1, so you haven't deleted anything really important.

Let's create an updated version of our WORK1 disk. We can do this either with the DISKCOPY command, or using the asterisk wildcard.

Single-drive and hard disk systems:

Insert the WORK1 disk in drive A: and have your WORK3 disk available. The WORK1 disk is your source disk, and WORK3 is your target disk.

Enter the following and follow the instructions on the screen:

```
COPY *.* B: <Enter>
```

Dual-drive systems:

Insert the WORK1 disk in drive A: and your WORK3 disk in drive B:. The WORK1 disk is your source disk, and WORK3 is your target disk.

Enter the following:

```
COPY *.* B: <Enter>
```

The above procedure copies all files on WORK1 to the WORK3 disk without destroying any existing files there. If any files already exist on the target disk under the same names as those on the source disk, COPY replaces all the existing files with the versions from the source disk.

4.1.4   Effectively placing the asterisk

The asterisk wildcard can replace whole words or even parts of words. When MS-DOS finds an asterisk in a filename, any combination of characters can be accepted. Insert your WORK1 disk in drive A: and enter the following sequences:

```
COPY CON MULLER.TXT<Enter>
text<Enter>
<Ctrl><Z>
<Enter>

COPY MULLER.TXT MEYER.TXT<Enter>
COPY MULLER.TXT BEIER.TXT<Enter>
COPY MULLER.TXT MAYER.TXT<Enter>
COPY MULLER.TXT METZGER.TXT<Enter>
```

You now have five files with the same file extension (.TXT). Using the procedure for your system, copy the files over to the WORK3 disk using the following sequence:

```
COPY *.TXT B:<Enter>
```

Look at the command syntax again. If you place an asterisk before the period, DOS accesses all files with the same extension.

The asterisk replaces all characters following it in either a filename or an extension. The following sequence would copy all files with the .TXT extension to drive B:, including LETTER.TXT (do not enter this sequence):

```
COPY *ULLER.TXT B:
```

And the following sequence would copy all files with extensions starting with .Q from drive A: to drive B: (do not enter this sequence):

```
COPY A:*.Q* B:
```

Summary

Commands related to file access can often use wildcards to replace part or all of a filename and file extension. The asterisk wildcard replaces groups of characters within a filename. For example, LETTER*.TXT affects all files with a .TXT extension, and filenames which begin with LETTER.

Letters following the wildcard are ignored. For example, the characters following this sequence are ignored:

COPY A:*RED.TXT B:

The above sequence is treated by MS-DOS as this:

COPY A:*.TXT B:

is identical to this sequence. Wildcards on either side of the period affects all files on a disk. For example, the following deletes all files on a disk:

DEL *.*

4.2   Finding files in a directory

Asterisks can serve one more purpose. We can display individual files from a directory with the help of asterisk wildcards and the `DIR FILENAME` command.

Insert the WORK1 disk in drive A: and enter the following:

`DIR LETTER*.*<Enter>`

This lists the directory's files beginning with `LETTER`:

```
Volume in drive A is WORK1
Directory of A:\

LETTER    BAK      143    3-09-89    9:19a
LETTER1   BAK      143    3-09-89    9:19a
LETTER2   BAK      143    3-09-89    9:19a
LETTER3   BAK      143    3-09-89    9:19a
LETTER4   BAK       15    3-09-89    3:02p
         5 File(s)    350208 bytes free
```

DIR FILENAME   `DIR  FILENAME` limits the directory to the files or file extensions requested. This can be very helpful when searching for files in longer directories.

Suppose you're only looking for one file on a disk. How can you see whether that file exists? `DIR FILENAME` can help.

Remove the WORK1 disk from the drive, and insert the BACKUP SYSTEM disk. Enter the following to display the entry for FORMAT, including its size and storage date:

`DIR FORMAT<Enter>`

4.3 The question mark wildcard

One other wildcard exists in addition to the asterisk. The question mark can replace single characters in filenames and extensions.

Remove the BACKUP SYSTEM disk from drive A: and insert WORK1 in drive A:. Let's search for the text file named MAYER.TXT. Enter:

```
DIR M?YER.TXT <Enter>
```

The directory lists two files—MAYER.TXT and MEYER.TXT. MS-DOS reads the question mark as any character.

Let's see if we can list both files to the screen. Enter the following:

```
TYPE M?YER.TXT<Enter>
```

the computer responds with:

```
Invalid filename or file not found
```

Unlike DIR and COPY, TYPE can only access one file at a time— wildcards are not allowed.

Summary

The question mark can be used as a wildcard for single characters.

Multiple question marks can also be used. Both of the following examples search a directory for files beginning with P and having extensions of .EXE:

```
DIR P*.EXE
DIR P???????.EXE
```

Wildcards do not function with commands that can only access one file at a time (e.g., TYPE).

4.4   The wide directory

Perhaps you're just searching for a filename, and really don't care to know the file size or last update. The DIR/W command displays the directory in a different format. The /W option displays the filenames and file extensions only in wide (multiple-filename) format.

Remove the WORK1 disk from drive A:. Insert the BACKUP SYSTEM disk and enter the following:

DIR/W<Enter>

Your directory will appear in a format similar to this (your filenames will probably be different from those appearing here):

```
Volume in drive A is 320_PC10-20

Directory of A:\

COMMAND  COM  ANSI      SYS  APPEND   COM  ASSIGN   COM  ATTRIB   EXE
FUNCTION BAK  CHKDSK    EXE  CONFIG   .SYS DEBUG    EXE  DISKCOMP EXE
DISKCOPY EXE  DRIVER    SYS  EDLIN    .EXE FIND     EXE  FORMAT   EXE
KEYBGR   COM  MODE      EXE  MORE     COM  PRINT    EXE  RAMDRIVE SYS
REPLACE  EXE  SORT      EXE  TREE     EXE  XCOPY    EXE  10030960
10031334      10041E1A       10041F4B       KEYBSP   COM  KEYBSU   COM
KEYBSV   COM  KEYBUK    COM  LABEL    EXE  MODE     EXE  MORE     COM
PRINT    EXE  RAMDRIVE  SYS  RECOVER  EXE  REPLACE  EXE  SORT     EXE
SUBST    EXE  SYS       COM  TREE     EXE  DEMO     COM  AUTOEXEC BAK
TODAY    BAT  FUNCTION  BAT  CRLF          DEBUG    DAT  NOTICBLK TXT
NOTICBLK BAK  DATIME$$  BAT  NOTICE   BAT  NOTICE   BAK  STZ      BAK
PRIINT   BAT  STZ       PRT  LOGIN    BAT  PRIINT   BAK  LOGBOOK  TXT
        60 file(s)       40960 Byte free
```

It does look completely different. The files are displayed in groups of five on a line, to allow you to read filenames more easily.

4.5   Sorted directories

We have one more directory display technique in store for you. Keep
the BACKUP SYSTEM disk in drive A:. Enter the following, but do
not press the <Enter> key yet:

DIR

Now, look on your keyboard for a key that looks something like this:

If you have such a key on your keyboard, press and hold a <Shift> key
then press this <\> key. If you don't have a key that looks like this,
press the key marked <NumLock> on your keyboard. A light will
probably go on on the keyboard, telling you that <NumLock> is
active. Press and hold the <Alt> key, then press <1><2><4> on the
numeric keypad, as if you were typing the number 124. Release the
<Alt> key.

Either process creates a I character, sometimes called a pipe character.
Next enter the word SORT so that the line looks like this (don't press
the <Enter> key yet):

DIR | SORT

Before pressing the <Enter> key, remove the BACKUP SYSTEM disk
from drive A:. Make sure that the disk isn't write protected: Remove
the tab or move the slider, depending on your disk format. Re-insert the
BACKUP SYSTEM disk in drive A:.

Press the <Enter> key. Nothing happens for about 15 seconds. Then all
the entries of your BACKUP SYSTEM disk are listed alphabetically.
Your directory listing will look different from the one listed below—we
included this one here for a general illustration:

```
      37 file(s)     45056 bytes free
Volume in drive A: has no name
Directory of A:\
ANSI     SYS    1651    7-07-86   12:00p
APPEND   COM    1725    7-07-86   12:00p
ASSIGN   COM    1523    7-07-86   12:00p
ATTRIB   EXE    8234    7-07-86   12:00p
AUTOEXEC BAK     448    1-02-80    1:45a
CHKDSK   EXE    9680    7-07-86   12:00p
COMMAND  COM   23612    7-07-86   12:00p
CONFIG   SYS      31    2-26-87   10:12a
CRLF              2    1-02-80    2:14a
DEBUG    EXE   15647    7-07-86   12:00p
DEMO     COM     256    1-02-80   12:50a
DISKCOPY EXE    4096    7-07-86   12:00p
DRIVER   SYS    1102    7-07-86   12:00p
EDLIN    EXE    7356    7-07-86   12:00p
FIND     EXE    6403    7-07-86   12:00p
FORMAT   EXE   11005    7-07-86   12:00p
LABEL    EXE    2750    7-07-86   12:00p
LOGBOOK  TXT      38    1-02-80    3:56p
LOGIN    BAT      38    1-02-80    3:41p
MODE     EXE   13928    7-07-86   12:00p
MORE     COM     282    7-07-86   12:00p
MORO     COM     282    7-07-86   12:00p
NOTICE   BAK     218    1-02-80    2:27a
NOTICE   BAT     210    1-02-80    2:30a
PRINT    EXE    8824    7-07-86   12:00p
QUILL    EXE    8824    7-07-86   12:00p
RAMDRIVE SYS    6462    7-07-86   12:00p
RAMESES  SYS    6462    7-07-86   12:00p
RECOVER  EXE    4145    7-07-86   12:00p
REPLACE  EXE    4852    7-07-86   12:00p
REPLICAT EXE    4852    7-07-86   12:00p
SORT     EXE    1914   28.05.86   12:00p
SUBST    EXE    9898    7-07-86   12:00p
SYS      COM    4607    7-07-86   12:00p
TREE     EXE    8588    7-07-86   12:00p
UTREE    EXE    8588    7-07-86   12:00p
XCOPY    EXE    5396    7-07-86   12:00p
```

DIR | SORT creates an alphabetically sorted directory. Enter the
DIR | SORT command again. As the directory lists, press the
<Ctrl><S> key. This stops the listing. Pressing <Ctrl><C> aborts the
listing.

Remove the BACKUP SYSTEM disk form drive A: and insert the
WORK1 disk. Enter:

DIR|SORT<Enter>

The PC responds with:

Bad command or filename

Don't panic. When you enter the DIR | SORT command, DOS looks for
the transient command called SORT. Since it can't find this command
on the WORK1 disk, the DIR command aborts.

Unlike the FORMAT and LABEL commands, DIR | SORT changes the
disk directory only temporarily.

Remove the WORK1 disk from drive A: and replace it with the
BACKUP SYSTEM disk. Enter the following (notice there is a space
between the words, and not a pipe):

DIR SORT<Enter>

The screen lists the program SORT.EXE. Preparing for the copying
process used by your system (insert the WORK1 disk in drive B: if you
have a two drive system), enter the following:

DIR B:|SORT<Enter>

The PC reads the SORT command from drive A: and sorts the directory
of the disk for drive B:. If you have a single-drive system or a hard disk
system, this requires some disk switching on your part.

The WORK1 disk directory will look something like this once the
SORT command finishes its task (don't panic if yours looks slightly
different):

```
                    23 file(s)      349184 bytes free

Volume in drive A, has the name WORK1
Directory of A:\

BEIER      TXT         6    3-09-89    3:49p
LETTER     BAK        48    3-09-89    9:19a
LETTER1    BAK        48    3-09-89    9:19a
LETTER2    BAK        48    3-09-89    9:19a
LETTER3    BAK        48    3-09-89    9:19a
LETTER4    BAK        14    3-09-89    3:02p
MALLWALK   TXT       106    3-09-89    6:20p
MAYER      TXT         6    3-09-89    4:57p
METZGER    TXT         6    3-09-89    3:49p
MEYER      TXT         6    3-09-89    3:57p
MILLER     TXT       167    3-09-89    6:21p
MULLER     TXT         6    3-09-89    3:49p
NEWLETT    TXT        48    3-09-89    9:19a
NOEXTEN1   TXT         6    3-09-89    3:33p
NOEXTEN2   TXT         6    3-09-89    3:33p
NOEXTEN3   TXT         6    3-09-89    3:33p
NOEXTEN4   TXT         6    3-09-89    3:33p
NOEXTEN5   TXT         6    3-09-89    3:33p
NOEXTEN6   TXT         6    3-09-89    3:33p
ROMELIST   TXT       150    3-09-89    9:11a
STORE      TXT        55    3-09-89    2:40p

TRIAL                129    3-09-89    2:43p
TRIXIE     TXT        88    3-09-89    3:19p
```

Summary

The disk directory can be displayed in forms other than the normal, scrolling version and the /P page format version. These other versions make the directory much easier to read, and help the user find filenames much more quickly.

First, the /W option displays the filenames and file extensions of a disk directory in wide format. File size, date and time information are suppressed, and the filenames appear in the directory listing five per line. The syntax:

DIR/W

The directory can be displayed in an alphabetically sorted form using the DIR command in combination with the pipe character and the transient command called SORT. The syntax is as follows:

DIR|SORT

The DIR|SORT command is only temporary—it makes no permanent changes to the disk directory.

4.6   Function keys

You have probably made more than enough typing errors during this book. MS-DOS seems to require a great deal of input, especially for more detailed tasks. For example, think of the line you entered from the last section which accessed the SORT command from drive A: and sorted the directory in drive B:.

```
DIR B:|SORT
```

Also, think about how exacting MS-DOS is. You can't place spaces in filenames:

```
COPY CON LANA RAE.TXT
```

Nor can you misspell anything:

```
DISCCOPY
```

These entries result in errors.

MS-DOS does exactly what you tell it to do—provided you tell it what it understands, in the way that it understands.

Now, let's select a problem command from what we've listed here, and explore error correction a little further. Place the WORK1 disk in drive A: and enter the following:

```
COPY CON LANA RAE.TXT<Enter>
```

The computer responds:

```
Invalid number of parameters
```

This means that MS-DOS doesn't like the space between LANA and RAE. You could enter the command all over again, this time without a space. Re-entering commands all the time can get pretty frustrating. Still, we want to create this file. What can you do to make this easier?

4.6.1 Command recall with the <F3> key

MS-DOS has some features to help. Before you do anything else with the keyboard, look for the function keys on your keyboard. The locations of these keys can vary with each PC—they may be on the left edge of your keyboard, or they may be on the top edge, running parallel to the number keys.

Look for the <F3> key. Press it and watch the screen. The following should appear:

```
COPY CON LANA RAE.TXT
```

Press the <Backspace> (<⇐>) key or the <Left arrow> cursor key to erase the text up to the space. The text should look like this (the black box is your cursor):

```
COPY CON LANA■
```

Enter the text RAE.TXT so that the line looks something like this:

```
COPY CON LANARAE.TXT■
```

The <F3> key retains the last command sequence entered, right or wrong. You can press <F3> to restore the command, edit the command so that it's correct, and press <Enter> to execute the command.

Press the <Enter> key to move to the next line and open the file. If you didn't really want to create this file after all, you can terminate any time by pressing <Ctrl><C>. Press <Ctrl><C> now to exit this file and return to the system prompt.

The <F3> key repeats the last command entered. This last command appears at the system prompt. You can edit the command using the <Backspace> or <Left arrow> key, or just press <Enter> to re-execute the command.

The <F3> key is particularly useful for displaying directories. For example, if you invoke DIR without being prepared, half the directory can scroll past before you get a chance to press <Ctrl><S> to pause the display. This is especially true for those of you who own AT models, which operate at very high execution speeds.

If you miss the display, no problem. Press <F3>, get your hand next to the <Ctrl> key and the <S> key, and press the <Enter> key to start the directory again.

These function keys each serve a function, as their names imply. The functions vary from program to program, and MS-DOS is no exception.

Let's experiment further with some variations on the DIR command. Remove the WORK1 disk from drive A: and replace it with the BACKUP SYSTEM disk. Enter the following:

DIR<Enter>

When the system prompt reappears, press the <F3> key to display the following:

DIR

Enter /P so that the command looks like this:

DIR/P

Press the <Enter> key to display the directory in page format.

When the system prompt reappears, press the <F3> key to display the following:

DIR/P

Use the <Backspace> or <Left arrow> key to delete the P. Enter W so that the command looks like this:

DIR/W

Press the <Enter> key to display the directory in wide format.

Make sure your printer is connected, filled with paper and turned on. Press <F3> to recall the DIR/W command. Delete the /W using the <Backspace> key or <Left arrow> key. Edit the command so that it looks like this:

DIR > PRN:

Press the <Enter> key to send the directory to the printer instead.

Remove the BACKUP SYSTEM disk and place the WORK1 disk in drive A:. Enter the following (this will cause an error—don't panic):

```
DIR TRIAD<Enter>
```

When the error appears, press the <F3> key to recall the command. Edit the line so that it looks like this:

```
DIR TRIAL
```

Press the <Enter> key to execute it.

4.6.2   Character recall with the <F1> key

One other function key offers editing help in MS-DOS. The <F1> key recalls the previous command, *one character at a time*. For example, enter the error we entered above:

```
COPY CON LANA RAE.TXT<Enter>
```

This results in the same error as before.

Now press the <F1> key and watch the screen at the system prompt. A C appears on the screen. Press the <F1> key again—an O appears. Keep pressing the <F1> key until the following text is on the screen (the black box represents your cursor):

```
COPY CON LANA■
```

Add the necessary characters so that the text looks like this:

```
COPY CON LANARAE.TXT■
```

Deleting characters
Since we had to press the <F1> key 13 times, this is of limited help in cases like this; the <F3> key would have been much more helpful. However, consider the times when you might make errors early on in the line. Enter the following:

```
COPPY CON LANARAE.TXT
```

The computer responds with:

```
Bad command or filename
```

Press <F1> until you get to the first P (the black box is your cursor):

COPY■

Look for the <Del> or <Delete> key (this is a different key from the <Backspace> key). Press the <Del> key, even though no other characters are visible to the right of the cursor. Now press the <F3> key and look at the result on the screen:

COPY CON LANARAE.TXT

Inserting characters

Press the <Enter> key, then press <Ctrl><C> to abort. Look again at the line you just entered. You can add a drive specifier to this line.

Press the <F1> key nine times to get the following:

COPY CON ■

Look on your keyboard for the <Insert> key. Press the <Insert> key and enter the letter B and a colon, so that the line looks like this:

COPY CON B:■

Press the <F3> key to recall the rest of the text:

COPY CON B:LANARAE.TXT

Press <Enter>, then press <Ctrl><C> to return to the system prompt.

The <F3> key only recalls the entire previous command if the cursor lies at the leftmost position of the command line. The status of this command changes every time you press <F1> to add single characters on the screen. Then the <F3> key displays the text starting at the current cursor position.

4.6.3   A <Ctrl><Z> shortcut with the <F6> key

The <F6> key also helps in editing. Press the <F3> key to displays the following:

COPY CON B:LANARAE.TXT

Press the <Enter> key and enter a few words:

Hello, Lana.<Enter>

We still need a <Ctrl><Z> and an <Enter> to close the file. Press the <F6> key. This automatically places a <Ctrl><Z> on the screen. If you press the <Enter> key, the file closes and goes to disk.

Summary

The function keys serve different purposes in different programs and environments. MS-DOS has three function keys available:

<F1>   Recalls each character of the last command entered, one character at a time.

<F3>   Recalls the last command entered, if no changes have been made to the current line.

<F6>   Enters a <Ctrl><Z> (important because it indicates the end of a file).

The <F1> and <F3> keys can be used in combination, for editing errors in a previous command. Errors may be edited using the <Del> key and the <Insert> key.

5.   The AUTOEXEC.BAT file

Now that you've learned some of the basic concepts of MS-DOS, we can take a close look at a file named AUTOEXEC.BAT, that can take care of a number of "housekeeping chores" when you turn on your PC. This chapter shows you what this file is, what it does, how to create your own AUTOEXEC.BAT file, and how you can configure it to do what you want it to do.

You will need the following for this chapter:

*   BACKUP SYSTEM disk

*   A blank disk

*   A label

*   felt-tip pen

5.1   AUTOEXEC.BAT: What is it?

This file, called AUTOEXEC.BAT, is a simple text file, just like the ones you've created yourself using the COPY CON command in the last few chapters. You may also remember a brief mention of *batch files* back in Section 1.5. There you created a batch file named MYFILE.BAT, which performed a few simple tasks when you entered its command name.

Batch files

Batch files execute a batch (group) of commands on your PC. They save you a great deal of typing time, since you only have to enter the commands once—when you create the batch file.

AUTOEXEC.BAT is actually an abbreviation for AUTOEXECute BATch file. This means that when you turn on your PC, MS-DOS searches for a file by this name, and automatically executes the commands contained in AUTOEXEC.BAT.

Now, you may or may not have an AUTOEXEC.BAT file on your BACKUP SYSTEM disk. If you have a hard disk, the odds are good that you do have one on the hard disk. Let's find out.

Disk check

Insert the BACKUP SYSTEM disk in drive A:. Turn on your monitor and PC. Do what you must to get to the system prompt (enter date or time, etc.). Make sure that the system prompt reads A>.

Enter the following:

```
DIR AUTOEXEC.BAT<Enter>
```

Watch the screen. If you have an AUTOEXEC.BAT file on the
BACKUP SYSTEM disk, the screen displays the following or a
similar message:

```
Volume in  drive A has no label
Directory of A:\
AUTOEXEC BAT       40  27.10.87   9.14
       1 file(s)        1024 bytes free
```

If you have no such file, the screen displays the following:

```
Volume in  drive A has no label
Directory of A:\
File not found
```

Hard disk: If you have a hard disk on your PC, and you don't have an
AUTOEXEC.BAT file on your BACKUP SYSTEM disk, enter the
following:

```
C:<Enter>
DIR AUTOEXEC.BAT<Enter>
```

There should be a file named AUTOEXEC.BAT on your hard disk.

All systems: **Do not touch the** AUTOEXEC.BAT **file on your hard disk or
on your BACKUP SYSTEM disk until you are totally
familiar with MS-DOS.** This file is vitally important to starting
up your PC. You can load both DOS and AUTOEXEC.BAT from drive
A: regardless of the system you have, which is what we'll do in this
chapter.

Even if you do have an AUTOEXEC.BAT file on your BACKUP
SYSTEM disk or hard disk, no matter. We're going to show you how
to create your own, using a backup of the BACKUP SYSTEM disk.

5.1.1   Creating an AUTOEXEC.BAT file

First, we need to make a copy of your BACKUP SYSTEM disk. This
backup gives us all the DOS commands available on the BACKUP
SYSTEM disk, and the option of creating an AUTOEXEC.BAT file
without risk.

Backing up

Make sure your system prompt reads A>. Place write protection on your BACKUP SYSTEM disk, using the procedure for your disk format (tab or slider). Insert your BACKUP SYSTEM disk in drive A:. Insert a blank disk in drive B: (dual-drive systems) or keep it close at hand (single-drive or hard disk systems).

Enter the following:

```
DISKCOPY A: B:<Enter>
```

Follow the instructions on the screen for your system.

When the process is done, take the duplicate disk and place a label on it. Take the felt-tip pen and label the disk DOS_WORK. Insert the DOS_WORK disk in drive A:. and enter the following:

```
LABEL<Enter>
```

When the screen prompts for a name, enter the following (the underline is usually <Shift><-->):

```
DOS_WORK<Enter>
```

This assigns the volume name DOS_WORK to the disk.

Leave the DOS_WORK disk in drive A:. Make sure the system prompt reads A>. If it doesn't, enter:

```
A:<Enter>
```

Creating an AUTOEXEC

Enter the following. We'll explain what you're doing as we go along. You've already read about most of these in Section 1.5:

```
COPY CON A:AUTOEXEC.BAT<Enter>
```

This creates the file AUTOEXEC.BAT on drive A:. Enter the following:

```
CLS<Enter>
```

This command should look familiar to you from Section 1.5, when you created the MYFILE.BAT file. The CLS command clears the screen. Enter the following:

```
VER<Enter>
```

The VER command displays the current version number of MS-DOS. Enter the following:

```
PROMPT $N$G<Enter>
```

PROMPT

The PROMPT command changes the appearance of the prompt. The $N parameter tells MS-DOS to display the current disk drive, while the $G parameter tells MS-DOS to display the > character ($G = Greater than). Enter the following:

```
DATE<Enter>
TIME<Enter>
```

These commands display the current system date and time. Each command also prompts the user for the current date and time: You can enter these or just press <Enter> to accept the system date and time as they stand. Enter the following:

```
<F6><Enter>
```

<F6> key

The <F6> key inserts a <Ctrl><Z> to indicate the end of file (you'll remember using this in Chapter 4). Pressing the <Enter> key saves the file to disk.

Now you have the same AUTOEXEC.BAT file on your DOS_WORK disk as we have on ours.

Enter the following to see a listing of the file:

```
TYPE A:AUTOEXEC.BAT<Enter>
```

The file should look like this on the screen:

```
CLS
VER
PROMPT $N$G
DATE
TIME
^Z
```

Testing

Now, switch off your computer for about ten seconds. Make sure that your DOS_WORK disk is in drive A:. Turn the computer back on and watch the screen. The computer should go through its usual startup process (testing memory, etc.).

As the computer starts, it checks drive A: for the `AUTOEXEC.BAT` file, and executes the commands contained in that file. It clears the screen, displays the version of MS-DOS in use, changes to the prompt requested, and asks you for the current date. Enter the date and press <Enter>. The computer then asks you for the current time. Enter the time and press <Enter>. Finally, the system prompt appears.

5.2 Changing AUTOEXEC.BAT

Now let's create another AUTOEXEC.BAT file. Enter the following:

```
COPY CON A:AUTOEXEC.BAT<Enter>
```

Now enter the following lines:

```
CLS<Enter>
PROMPT $N: Please input something -}<Enter>
<F6><Enter>
```

This overwrites the AUTOEXEC.BAT file currently on the disk with this new file.

Switch off your computer for about ten seconds. Make sure that your DOS_WORK disk is in drive A:. Turn the computer back on and watch the screen. The computer should go through its usual startup process (testing memory, etc.).

As the computer starts, it checks drive A: for the AUTOEXEC.BAT file, and executes the commands contained in that file. It clears the screen and displays a <u>new</u> system prompt—one that you just designed:

```
A: Please input something -}
```

PROMPT
Unlike the demonstration of PROMPT in Chapter 1, placing the PROMPT command in AUTOEXEC.BAT invokes a custom system prompt every time you start the system with the DOS_WORK disk in drive A:.You may have noticed that we omitted the DATE and TIME commands, as well as the VER command. You can manually enter the DATE and TIME commands to enter the current date and time. And since you already know which version of MS-DOS you have by now, you don't really need the VER command. You can enter it manually if you've forgotten.

Summary
Batch files are text files which let you execute multiple commands just by typing the name of the batch file. The PC searches for AUTOEXEC.BAT when turned on. The PC then automatically executes the AUTOEXEC.BAT file, if one exists. AUTOEXEC.BAT can be used to clear the screen, display the current version of MS-DOS, prompt the user for the current date and time, and even redefine the appearance of the system prompt.

5.3   Resetting your computer

Enter the following lines to create a new AUTOEXEC.BAT file. Make sure you include a space after the exclamation point in the second line:

```
COPY CON A:AUTOEXEC.BAT<Enter>
CLS<Enter>
PROMPT $N$G Please input something! <Enter>
VER<Enter>
DATE<Enter>
TIME<Enter>
<F6><Enter>
```

This overwrites the old AUTOEXEC.BAT file.

Don't switch off your computer yet. In fact, you don't have to switch it off at all to test this batch file. You can actually *reset* the computer to its starting condition without turning it off. The manufacturers include this option on PCs and PC compatibles to help alleviate wear and tear on computer and monitor alike.

Reset   Press and hold the <Ctrl> and <Alt> keys. While holding these two keys, press the <Del> key and release all three keys. This process is called "pressing Control-Alt-Delete" and resets the computer. The screen clears and the PC executes a shorter startup sequence than it does when you turn it on (e.g., no memory test, etc.). The PC then executes the AUTOEXEC.BAT file in sequence.

Warm start   This reset, also called a *warm start*, can be used at almost any time to restart the computer. Turning the computer off and on is called a *cold start*.

5.4   The ECHO command

You've noticed that the commands appear on the screen as the AUTOEXEC.BAT file executes. It looks rather sloppy, but we can fix that.

ECHO OFF The ECHO command serves many purposes in batch file creation. One important purpose is disabling the display of command execution in batch files, called ECHO OFF.

Make sure your DOS_WORK disk is still in drive A:. Enter the following:

```
COPY CON A:AUTOEXEC.BAT<Enter>
ECHO OFF<Enter>
PROMPT $N$G<Enter>
TIME<Enter>
DATE<Enter>
<F6><Enter>
```

Press <Control><Alt><Del> to reset the computer. The computer resets and ECHO OFF appears on the screen for a moment. Then the time prompt appears immediately. Press the <Enter> key. The date prompt appears immediately. Press the <Enter> key to get to the system prompt.

ECHO ECHO OFF suppresses the display of batch file commands as they execute. But ECHO itself has many powerful capabilities, such as text display.

Enter the following lines:

```
COPY CON A:AUTOEXEC.BAT<Enter>
ECHO OFF<Enter>
PROMPT $N$G<Enter>
CLS<Enter>
ECHO Hello, User.<Enter>
ECHO Ready when you are.<Enter>
<F6><Enter>
```

Press <Ctrl><Alt><Del> and watch the screen. ECHO OFF appears briefly and then the screen clears. The following appears in the upper left corner of the screen:

```
Hello, User.
Ready when you are.
A>
```

These ECHO commands displayed these messages on the screen.

Summary

The PC can usually be reset or warm started by pressing the <Ctrl><Alt><Del> keys simultaneously. This is faster and places much less stress on the computer than turning it off and on.

The ECHO command serves a number of purposes in batch files, such as text display and suppressing the display of batch file command names as they execute.

6.   Introduction to EDLIN

So far, we've created a number of text files. We've had you enter one particular file many times over. You're probably wondering by now if there isn't a way to change a file, rather than re-inventing the wheel by retyping it. There is.

This chapter shows you the basics of operating a program called EDLIN, included with almost every MS-DOS system. EDLIN is a simple *line editor* which allows you to create new text files and *edit* (modify) existing ones. This is much simpler than re-entering a file from square one using COPY CON.

You will need the following for this chapter:

• DOS_WORK disk

• EDLIN (should be on your DOS_WORK disk: If not, check your second DOS disk for it and use the COPY command to copy it over)

6.1   Editing the AUTOEXEC.BAT file

There's an easier way to create, list and edit files. Make sure that the DOS_WORK disk is in drive A:, and that the system prompt currently reads A>. Enter the following:

```
TYPE A:AUTOEXEC.BAT<Enter>
```

The screen displays the following file which you entered at the end of Chapter 5:

```
ECHO OFF
PROMPT $N$G
CLS
ECHO Hello, User.
ECHO Ready when you are.
```

Now enter:

```
DIR EDLIN<Enter>
```

The directory should display the following or a similar message:

```
Volume in drive A: is DOS_WORK
Directory of A:\

EDLIN    EXE   8018  11-22-86   8:00a
          1 File(s)    1024 bytes free
```

Enter the following:

```
EDLIN A:AUTOEXEC.BAT<Enter>
```

The following appears on the screen:

```
End of input file
*
```

A blinking cursor appears to the right of the asterisk. No system prompt or other data appears.

6.1.1   Editing lines with EDLIN

You cannot just enter anything in EDLIN. Enter the following:

```
What is this?<Enter>
```

The PC responds with this or a similar message:

```
Entry error
```

L

Like MS-DOS, EDLIN accepts commands that it can comprehend. For example, EDLIN will list a file if you enter the L command. Enter the following:

```
L<Enter>
```

The following lines appear, indented from the left border of the screen:

```
1:*ECHO OFF
2: PROMPT $N$G
3: CLS
4: ECHO Hello, User.
5: ECHO Ready when you are.
```

EDLIN displays a file line by line and numbers these lines. The line numbers only appear for your reference in EDLIN. If you created a file in EDLIN, exited EDLIN and used the TYPE command to list the file, these line numbers would not appear on the screen.

Enter the following (notice the number precedes the command letter):

4L<Enter>

n L

EDLIN lists lines 4 and 5 of the file. Entering L without any other parameters displays the entire file on the screen.

D

Suppose you don't like the line that says Ready when you are. We can delete it using the D command. Enter:

5D<Enter>

Nothing seems to happen. Now enter the following, which lists the entire file on the screen:

L<Enter>

The following text appears on the screen, minus line 5:

```
1:*ECHO OFF
2: PROMPT $N$G
3: CLS
4: ECHO Hello, User.
```

The D stands for DELETE. Entering D without any other parameters returns an error message. Entering a number with D deletes that line from the file. The 5D command used above deletes line 5 from the file.

I

Suppose you change your mind, and you like the Ready when you are line. The I (Insert) command lets you insert lines in a text file. Enter the following:

I<Enter>

The screen will display a 5, a colon and an asterisk. The asterisk acts as a placeholder, marking a line where editing most recently took place. This asterisk will move about the file, but will not be saved when you quit EDLIN. Now enter the following:

ECHO Ready when you are.<Enter>

Press <Enter>. EDLIN immediately displays a line number 6, a colon and an asterisk. Enter the following:

111

```
ECHO --<Enter>
```

EDLIN displays a 7, a colon and an asterisk. Enter the following:

```
ECHO I'll wait until you enter something.<Enter>
```

EDLIN displays an 8, a colon and an asterisk. Enter the following:

```
ECHO --<Enter>
```

EDLIN displays a 9, a colon and an asterisk. Enter the following:

```
ECHO Please enter something!<Enter>
```

A tenth line appears on the screen. Press <Ctrl><Z> or <F6>, then press the <Enter> key. The cursor jumps to the *command prompt* (the asterisk at the left border of the screen).

Press <L><Enter> to see the entire file listing:

```
1:*ECHO OFF
2: PROMPT $N$G
3: CLS
4: ECHO Hello, User.
5: ECHO Ready when you are.
6: ECHO --
7: ECHO I'll wait until you enter something.
8: ECHO --
9: ECHO Please enter something!
```

If you forgot an ECHO in lines 4 to 9, enter the line number and <Enter> to display the problem line. Enter the correct command. Press <F6><Enter> to return to the command prompt.

E   This file still isn't saved to disk. Enter the following:

```
E<Enter>
```

The E (END EDIT) command saves the file and returns you to the system prompt.

Press <Ctrl><Alt><Del> to reset the machine. The screen clears and the following appears on the screen:

```
Hello, User.
Ready when you are.
—
I'll wait until you enter something.
—
Please enter something!

A>
```

Enter the following:

```
DIR AUTOEXEC.*<Enter>
```

You'll find two files named AUTOEXEC, but with two different extensions. The one has a .BAT extension, which is to be expected. However, another file exists under the same name but with a .BAK extension. EDLIN automatically creates a .BAK (BAcKup) file when someone edits a file in EDLIN. Enter the following:

```
EDLIN A:AUTOEXEC.BAK<Enter>
```

The following or a similar error message appears on the screen:

```
Cannot edit .BAK file--rename file
```

Let's use the TYPE command to check out this backup file. Enter the following:

```
TYPE A:AUTOEXEC.BAK
ECHO OFF
PROMPT $N$G
CLS
ECHO Hello, User.
ECHO Ready when you are.
```

That was the AUTOEXEC.BAT file before you made changes. When you change a file with EDLIN and save it again, the previous version is backed up under the filename FILENAME.BAK. If for some reason you want to use the old file again, you can just rename it with: RENAME FILENAME.BAK FILENAME.NEW. Then you can access it from EDLIN.

6.1.2   Inserting lines with EDLIN

To find out how a file can be changed further with EDLIN, enter:

EDLIN A:AUTOEXEC.BAT<Enter>

We learned how to add lines to the end of a file. Now let's add lines to the midpoint of the file. Enter the following to display the file:

L<Enter>

The file appears:

```
1:*ECHO OFF
2: PROMPT $N$G
3: CLS
4: ECHO Hello, User.
5: ECHO Ready when you are.
6: ECHO --
7: ECHO I'll wait until you enter something.
8: ECHO --
9: ECHO Please enter something!
```

Enter the following to insert a line before line 5:

5I<Enter>

EDLIN displays 5: * and the cursor. Enter the following:

```
ECHO I am your new PC.<Enter>
<F6><Enter>
```

The new line 5 forces the old line 5 and any subsequent lines to shift "down." Entering <L><Enter> displays the following:

```
1:*ECHO OFF
2: PROMPT $N$G
3: CLS
4: ECHO Hello, User.
5: ECHO I am your new PC.
6: ECHO Ready when you are.
7: ECHO --
8: ECHO I'll wait until you enter something.
9: ECHO --
10: ECHO Please enter something!
```

Press <E><Enter> to end the edit and return to the system prompt.

6.1.3   Calling AUTOEXEC.BAT direct

Instead of resetting the computer, you can call AUTOEXEC.BAT direct
from the system prompt. Enter:

AUTOEXEC<Enter>

The computer executes all the commands in the AUTOEXEC.BAT file
in sequence.

Summary

EDLIN is a primitive line editor that lets you create and edit text files.
You can invoke the editor by entering EDLIN FILENAME.EXT.

The basic EDLIN commands you learned here are as follows:

L   Lists lines in a file. Entering <L><Enter> without any
          other parameters lists the entire file. Entering <nL><Enter>
          (where n = a line number) lists the file from line n to the
          end of the file. An asterisk appears in the line most recently
          edited.

I   Inserts lines in a file. Entering <I><Enter> without any
          other parameters lets you insert lines at the line number
          containing the asterisk. Entering <nI><Enter> (where n = a
          line number) lets you insert lines starting at line n. Any
          line numbers higher than the line being inserted are shifted
          down accordingly.

<F6>   (or <Ctrl><C>) Ends input.

E   Saves the original file with a .BAK extension, ends editing,
          saves the edited file and returns you to the system prompt.

D   Deletes lines. Entering <nD><Enter> (where n = a line
          number) deletes line number n. Entering <D><Enter>
          without any other parameters results in an error message.

6.2   File maintenance with EDLIN

EDLIN can also be used in cases where you previously used COPY
CON filename. This is true—EDLIN can be used for general text
editing, with more possibilities for editing than COPY CON allowed.

6.2.1   Editing files created with COPY   CON

Your WORK1 disk contains a number of text files that you created
earlier, including the file ROMELIST.TXT. Remove the DOS_WORK
disk from drive A:. Insert the WORK1 disk in drive A: and enter:

TYPE A:ROMELIST.TXT<Enter>

After a short time the following appears on the screen:

```
J. E. Fisher, Rome: Enjoying it More (J.R.R. Pub)
- , Yet Another Melting Pot-Rome
J. W. Schentzow, Knowing and Loving Rome (Random Access House)
```

Thanks to EDLIN you can easily modify this file. Make sure your
DOS_WORK disk is in drive A:, and that the system prompt indicates
drive A:. If you have two disk drives, insert the WORK1 disk into drive
B:—if not, just keep it close at hand. Enter the following:

COPY EDLIN.COM B:<Enter>

Follow the instructions on the screen, if any (single and hard disk
systems will ask you to do some disk switching).

Make sure that the WORK1 disk is in drive A:. Enter the following:

EDLIN ROMELIST.TXT (<Enter>)

you get the familiar display consisting of:

```
End of input file
*
```

Press <L><Enter> to get the following display:

```
1: *J. E. Fisher, Rome: Enjoying it More (J.R.R. Pub)
2: - , Yet Another Melting Pot-Rome
3: J. W. Schentzow, Knowing and Loving Rome (Random Access House)
```

This list can be easily changed. Enter the following:

```
4I<Enter>
```

This lets you insert a fourth line. Enter:

```
4: Franco Barelli, Rome. Art and Culture of the "Eternal City"<Enter>
5: <F6><Enter>
```

Press <E><Enter> to overwrite the old file and exit.

6.2.2   Creating a new file with EDLIN

Here is an example to demonstrate how to use EDLIN as a text editor, a program for creating text and editing on the screen.

You're preparing for your vacation in Rome. Since you promised postcards to lots of friends, you'll need some way of organizing their addresses.

Maybe your idea of organizing your address file is to write them on several pieces of paper. Slips of paper can get lost too easily. EDLIN can be used to organize and update these addresses.

Make sure the WORK1 disk is in drive A: and that the system prompt indicates drive A:. Enter:

```
EDLIN A:ADDRESS.TXT <Enter>
```

EDLIN reports with:

```
New file
*
```

Enter:

```
I<Enter>
```

The 1 : * prompt appears. Enter the following:

```
1: Andrew Bailey, 325 Washington Street, Salt Lake City, UT, 75680<Enter>
2: Jill Martin, 788 N. Elm Street, San Diego, CA, 94008<Enter>
3: Bill Remington, 104 Ocean View, Santa Barbara, CA, 94007<Enter>
4: Marsha and Elliot Samuels, 55 Gladiola, San Antonio, TX, 65925<Enter>
5: Jackie Smith, 871 West Samuels, Orlando, FL, 53290<Enter>
```

6: Michael Taylor, 2234 Market Ave, Cincinnati, OH, 44631<Enter>

7: Bob Willis, 543 Grand Ave., Santa Barbara, CA 94007<Enter>

8: <F6><Enter>

Press <E> <Enter> to save the file and exit to the system prompt.

You can also leave EDLIN without saving the data. Enter:

EDLIN JUNK.TXT<Enter>

The prompt New file appears. Enter <Q><Enter>. EDLIN asks:

Abort edit (Y/N)?

Enter <Y> to return to the system prompt.

6.2.3   Printing with EDLIN

Now you can print your address file. The simplest method would be to redirect the data to the printer with <Ctrl> and <PrtSc>, then enter TYPE ADDRESS.TXT. The following is another method of printing. Make sure your printer is connected, on and filled with paper. Enter:

COPY ADDRESS.TXT PRN

Summary

Entering EDLIN FILENAME invokes EDLIN. The file can be new or already in existence. EDLIN.COM must be available on disk, since EDLIN is a transient DOS command.

Entering <I><Enter> allows you to write date to a new file.

Files created from EDLIN can be printed using COPY FILENAME.EXT PRN.

You can leave EDLIN without saving text from the command prompt by entering <Q><Enter>. EDLIN asks if you want to abort the edit. Pressing <Y> returns you to the DOS system prompt. Pressing <N> keeps you in EDLIN.

6.3   Special capabilities of EDLIN

This section shows that EDLIN can do much more than just load, save and edit files. Once you finish the basic steps of using EDLIN with the PC, you'll probably upgrade to using true word processing applications for writing and editing text files. EDLIN is very primitive compared to most word processors on the market, so we're going to only show you EDLIN's capabilities in brief.

6.3.1   Replacing characters and words with EDLIN

Let's reload the ADDRESS.TXT file. Enter:

EDLIN ADDRESS.TXT<Enter>

Enter:

L<Enter>

The listing again appears:

```
1: Andrew Bailey, 325 Washington Street, Salt Lake City, UT , 75680
2: Jill Martin, 788 N. Elm Street, San Diego, CA, 94008
3: Bill Remington, 104 Ocean View, Santa Barbara, CA, 94007
4: Marsha and Elliot Samuels, 55 Gladiola, San Antonio, TX , 65925
5: Jackie Smith, 871 West Samuels, Orlando, FL, 53290
6: Michael Taylor, 2234 Market Ave., Cincinnati, OH, 44631
7: Bob Willis, 543 Grand Ave, Santa Barbara, CA, 94007
```

Read through the list. The street name in Jackie Smith's address should be "Samuel," not "Samuels". EDLIN lets you make the change easily.

Enter the following (press the keys as stated):

5,5?RSamuels<F6>Samuel<Enter>

The system responds:

```
5: Jackie Smith, 871 West Samuel, Orlando, FL, 53290
O.K.?
```

Press <Y> to get the command prompt. Enter <5L><Enter> to see the corrected line.

You could get this replacement to cover the entire range by entering the command so that it would cover the beginning to the ending text lines. For example, the below command changes all "Samuels" references in the text into "Samuel", making line 4 incorrect (don't enter this):

    1,7?RSamuels<F6>Samuel<Enter>

If the two numbers at the beginning of the command are identical, only that line is changed, as you saw above.

After reading through your list you realize that, because she was recently married, Jill Martin's last name should be changed to Sanford. Enter:

    2,2?RMartin<F6>Sanford

The name is changed to:

    2: Jill Sanford, 788 N. Elm Street, San Diego, CA, 94008

6.3.2   Moving lines with EDLIN

Since you changed Jill's last name, the list is no longer in alphabetical order. EDLIN contains a command for moving lines.

Enter the following:

    2,2,5m<Enter>

M

M (MOVE) moves the first and last line (2,2,) to the new location (5). <L><Enter> displays the following:

    1: Andrew Bailey, 325 Washington Street, Salt Lake City, UT, 75680
    2: Bill Remington, 104 Ocean View, Santa Barbara, CA, 94007
    3: Marsha and Elliot Samuels, 55 Gladiola, San Antonio, TX, 65925
    4: Jill Sanford, 788 N. Elm Street, San Diego, CA, 94008
    5: Jackie Smith, 871 West Samuel, Orlando, FL, 53290
    6: Michael Taylor, 2234 Market Ave., Cincinnati, OH, 44631
    7: Bob Willis, 543 Grand Ave., Santa Barbara, CA, 94007

6.3.3   Copying lines with EDLIN

You can also copy a line. For example, if you have a long list of addresses and you want to copy the addresses of people who have first priority at getting a card to the front of the list.

c

Enter:

5,5,1c<Enter>

This instructs EDLIN to copy everything from the fifth line to the fifth line up to line 1:

```
1: Jackie Smith, 871 West Samuel, Orlando, FL, 53290
2: Andrew Bailey, 325 Washington Street, Salt Lake City, UT, 75680
3: Bill Remington, 104 Ocean View, Santa Barbara, CA, 94007
4: Marsha and Elliot Samuels, 55 Gladiola, San Antonio, TX, 65925
5: Jill Sanford, 788 N. Elm Street, San Diego, CA, 94008
6: Jackie Smith, 871 West Samuel, Orlando, FL, 53290
7: Michael Taylor, 2234 Market Ave., Cincinnati, OH, 44631
8: Bob Willis, 543 Grand Ave., Santa Barbara, CA, 94007
```

Now you can add another name to the beginning:

Enter:

5,5,1c

The result is:

```
1: Jackie Smith, 871 West Samuel, Orlando, FL, 53290
2: Jill Sanford, 788 N. Elm Street, San Diego, CA, 94008
3: Andrew Bailey, 325 Washington Street, Salt Lake City, UT, 75680
4: Bill Remington, 104 Ocean View, Santa Barbara, CA, 94007
5: Marsha and Elliot Samuels, 55 Gladiola, San Antonio, TX, 65925
6: Jill Sanford, 788 N. Elm Street, San Diego, CA, 94008
7: Jackie Smith, 871 West Samuel, Orlando, FL, 53290
8: Michael Taylor, 2234 Market Ave., Cincinnati, OH, 44631
9: Bob Willis, 543 Grand Ave., Santa Barbara, CA, 94007
```

To seperate the lines that were taken out of the alphabetical list insert a line consisting of equal signs. Enter:

```
3I<Enter>
========================================================<Enter>
<F6><Enter>
```

```
 1: Jackie Smith, 871 West Samuel, Orlando, Fl, 53290
 2: Jill Sanford, 788 N. Elm Street, San Diego, CA, 94008
 3: ========================================================
 4: Andrew Bailey, 325 Washington Street, Salt Lake City, UT, 75680
 5: Bill Remington, 104 Ocean View, Santa Barbara, CA, 94007
 6: Marsha and Elliot Samuels, 55 Gladiola, San Antonio, TX, 65925
 7: Jill Sanford, 788 N. Elm Street, San Diego, CA, 94008
 8: Jackie Smith, 871 West Samuel, Orlando, FL, 53290
 9: Michael Taylor, 2234 Market Ave., Cincinnati, OH, 44631
10: Bob Willis, 543 Grand Ave., Santa Barbara, CA, 94007
```

Press <E><Enter> to save the file and exit EDLIN.

6.3.4   Displaying and deleting lines

Finally, here are some hints to use if your address list becomes too long. If you want to display single lines, you can enter:

5,9L

This instructs EDLIN to display lines 5 through 9.

The <D> command could be used to delete multiple lines:

11,15D

6.4   Review

Here's what we learned about EDLIN:

EDLIN is a primitive line editor, which can be used for entering, saving and editing text files.

The EDLIN command set covered in this chapter consisted of the following:

C   Copies lines from one location in a file to another.

D   Deletes lines.

E   Ends edit, saves file and returns to DOS.

I   Inserts lines.

L   Lists lines.

M   Moves lines from one location in a file to another.

Q   Quits EDLIN without saving edit.

R   Replaces one text with another, either in individual lines, ranges of lines, or entire files.

7.   Multiple directories

As you learned in Chapter 6 you can create a lot of files quickly with
EDLIN. But before you start writing letters to all of your friends, we
want to show you how to keep your disk files in order.

For this chapter you will need:

*   Your BACKUP SYSTEM disk

*   A blank disk

*   Label

*   Felt-tip pen

7.1   Hard disks

A regular floppy disk can store only so much data. This keeps the
number of files low, and makes it easier for you to keep track of files.

However, 1983 saw the development of the hard disk drive for the
storage of data. With this new method of storing data came new
capabilities, but also some problems. Whereas 5-1/4" disks could only
hold 360K and only about 100 files, the hard disk drive provided a
storage capacity 30 times larger, allowing up to 3,000 files.

Trying to find one file out of 3,000 could take quite a bit of time and
patience. Because of this new hardware capability, Microsoft had to
expand MS-DOS to provide space for more data, and better
organization. One example of this expansion can be seen in MS-DOS
Version 2.0, which included the invention of the *HFS (hierarchical file
structure)*.

7.2 Hierarchical file structure

The best way to explain HFS is to give you some illustrations of how it works. If you don't have a hard disk, you may be tempted to skip this section. Don't. The concepts explained here will work just as well for floppy disks as they do for hard disks. Read this, particularly if you have a PC compatible that uses 3-1/2" disk drives, since the memory capacity of that disk format can be kept organized using HFS.

Imagine a disk drive and a disk. Let's assume that you want to store on this disk your correspondence with various people. You could store all your letters on this disk. However, a filename like BIRTHDAY.TXT won't tell you if you sent a birthday letter to William Sullivan or Gary Moore. Plus, you might have trouble finding the file of the last letter you sent to Larry Markey.

If you didn't have a computer, you'd organize your letters in a desk by putting each letter in a different drawer according to the person or occasion. MS-DOS can perform the same task, in a way. It allows you to create "drawers" called *subdirectories* on a disk or hard disk. These subdirectories, as the name implies, act as directories within directories. You can access these subdirectories and the files they contain—provided that you use the correct commands.

Three important commands are used for creating, moving into and deleting subdirectories:

MKDIR or MD (MaKeDIRectory or Make Directory)—for creating a directory or subdirectory.

CHDIR or CD (CHangeDIRectory or Change Directory)—for moving into a directory or subdirectory.

RMDIR or RD (ReMoveDIRectory or Remove Directory)—for deleting a directory or subdirectory containing no data.

7.2.1 Creating directories

Insert your BACKUP SYSTEM disk in drive A:. Enter the following to invoke the FORMAT command:

```
FORMAT A:/V<Enter>
```

Insert a blank disk in drive A: when the screen instructs you to, and
follow the format instructions. When the screen prompts you for a
volume name, enter:

```
DIR_WORK<Enter>
```

Wait until the system prompt appears. Enter the following lines (if the
PC gives you a `Bad command or filename` error, enter `MKDIR`
instead of `MD`):

```
MD GARY<Enter>
MD WILLIAM<Enter>
MD LARRY<Enter>
```

Now enter the `DIR` command to view your PC.

```
Volume in drive A is DIR_WORK
Directory of A:

GARY          <DIR>      3-09-87   3:23p
WILLIAM       <DIR>      3-09-87   3:23p
LARRY         <DIR>      3-09-87   3:23p
        3 File(s)   349184 bytes free
```

At first it seems like the PC has created three files using these three
commands. But no file size appears. Instead of the number of bytes
there is a `<DIR>`. Let's get a closer look at these files.

Enter:

```
DIR GARY<Enter>
```

If `GARY` were the name of a file, the PC would list the file's name, size
and creation/most recent access date. Instead, the PC displays two lines
with one and two dots as filenames and the word `<DIR>`, as shown
here:

```
Volume in drive A is DIR_WORK
Directory of A:\GARY

.             <DIR>      3-09-87   3:23p
..            <DIR>      3-09-87   3:23p
        2 File(s)   349184 bytes free
```

7.2.2   Changing from one directory to another

The three MD commands created the drawers on the disk. We can prove this with the following test.

Enter:

```
CD GARY<Enter>
DIR<Enter>
Volume in drive A is DIR_WORK
Directory of A:\GARY

    .             <DIR>      3-09-87   3:23p
    ..            <DIR>      3-09-87   3:23p
            2 File(s)   349184 bytes free
```

Again the PC shows the two files with the dots. It usually would have displayed GARY, WILLIAM and LARRY. The CD GARY command places us in the GARY directory, and the WILLIAM and LARRY directories do not exist within the GARY directory. This is exactly what we wanted to do. To get out of the drawer again, enter:

```
CD ..<Enter>
```

Let's clarify the above input: Enter CD, a space and two periods.

Now when you enter a DIR command the screen displays all three directory names. The two periods tell MS-DOS that you want to move up by one level in the directory. Moving up by levels bring you closer to the *root directory* (main directory).

Let's discuss CD a little further. How do you specify which directory you want? When in the root (main) directory, you specify the name of the directory to which you want to move (GARY in the case above). To move back to the previous level, you enter CD, a space and two periods.

This subsection showed you how to move from the root directory to a lower directory level, and back up to the root directory. Next we'll discuss the topic of directories within directories.

Summary   The MD command (sometimes called MKDIR; both are abbreviations for Make Directory) creates a separate directory with the specified name on the specified disk.

The CD command (an abbreviation for Change Directory) moves to the specified directory, similar to entering a drive specifier.

7.2.3   Subdirectories

Think of the desk and drawer concept we described above. You don't just stuff most letters into drawers, unless you write very little correspondence. Your drawers stay organized if you use folders to hold your letters. That way, you can keep letters to each person in their own folders. The folders help you easily find these letters.

MS-DOS allows you to keep directories within directories. These *subdirectories* are created, accessed and removed in the same way you worked with the GARY, WILLIAM and LARRY directories above.

Currently you should be in the root directory of the DIR_WORK disk. If you enter the DIR command, the screen should display the GARY, WILLIAM and LARRY directories. If these names do not appear, enter:

```
CD ..<Enter>
DIR<Enter>
```

We're going to create two subdirectories named OCCUP (short for occupation) and PRIVATE within the GARY directory. Enter:

```
CD GARY<Enter>
```

This moves you into the GARY directory. Now enter:

```
MD OCCUP<Enter>
MD PRIVATE<Enter>
```

You used the MD command earlier to create the GARY, WILLIAM and LARRY directories. If you enter DIR now, the two new directories are displayed in addition to the periods representing the existing ones on the "upper level:"

```
Volume in drive A is DIR_WORK
Directory of A:\GARY

.               <DIR>        3-09-87   3:23p
..              <DIR>        3-09-87   3:23p
OCCUP           <DIR>        3-11-87  11:30a
PRIVATE         <DIR>        3-11-87  11:30a
        4 File(s)   347136 bytes free
```

To change the PRIVATE directory to the current directory, enter:

```
CD PRIVATE<Enter>
```

Use the DIR command to check your current location. The volume label should list this directory as PRIVATE.

7.2.4   Moving between directories

Now, suppose we want to change to the WILLIAM directory from the PRIVATE directory. Logic would tell us to enter the following (be prepared for an error):

```
CD WILLIAM<Enter>
```

The PC responds with this or a similar message:

```
Invalid Directory
```

This tells us that the PC cannot find a directory named WILLIAM. This is because the WILLIAM directory is in a different directory level of the disk from the PRIVATE subdirectory.

We can use two methods to change to the WILLIAM directory from the PRIVATE directory:

Single steps   We can move up one directory at a time:

```
CD ..<Enter>
CD ..<Enter>
CD WILLIAM<Enter>
```

This moves us up to the GARY directory, then to the root directory, then to the WILLIAM directory, in that order. This is a fairly roundabout method.

Paths   We can use *paths* to move rapidly from directory to directory. A few added characters can move us in one line to the WILLIAM directory from the PRIVATE directory.

If you followed the instructions above, you should be in the WILLIAM directory. If not, please change to the WILLIAM directory now.

Enter the following to return to the PRIVATE directory, using the process described above:

```
CD ..<Enter>
CD GARY<Enter>
CD PRIVATE<Enter>
```

Now enter the following line:

```
CD A:\WILLIAM<Enter>
```

No error. The A: tells MS-DOS to look in drive A:. The backslash character (\) which immediately follows the colon tells MS-DOS to return to the root directory and move to the directory named WILLIAM.

Now let's use paths (backslashes) to change to the PRIVATE directory. Enter:

```
CD A:\GARY\PRIVATE<Enter>
```

This instructs the PC to look in drive A:, move from the root directory to the GARY directory, then make the PRIVATE directory the current directory.

7.2.5   PROMPT $P

You'll remember working with the PROMPT command earlier in this book. You can instruct MS-DOS to display the current directory in a prompt. Enter:

```
PROMPT $P$G<Enter>
```

The $P tells the system to display the current disk path, and the $G displays the greater than character. If you're still in the PRIVATE directory, the prompt should look like this:

```
A:\GARY\PRIVATE>
```

Summary   The data structure on the disk is similar to the roots of a tree. Starting at the root directory (ground level), you can have files and directories as extensions of the root directory. Directories can contain files and subdirectories (other directories).

CD NAME changes the directory to the NAME directory, provided that the NAME directory is directly accessible from the current directory. CD .. moves the directory structure up by one level. The CD NAME and CD .. commands are relative to the current directory.

A backslash helps indicate the complete disk path, allowing rapid changes between directories in one command. CD \ returns the system to the root directory.

7.2.6 Subdirectories: A practical application

You know how to create subdirectories and how to move between different levels, but you still need to learn practical uses for this knowledge. We'll now store files in various directories, delete these files and copy them from one directory to another.

Before we continue, here are some reasons why experienced PC users like working with subdirectories:

• Readability. This is important for hard disk systems, because searching a large directory can be difficult. Even on floppy disk systems, a disk with 100 filenames can present problems when trying to find one file. If you own a PC with one drive and want to create a working disk for word processing, this disk would contain the word processor, files you generated using the word processor, and frequently used DOS commands. However, the search for the text files could be very time consuming. Instead, you could create three directories named DOS, PRG and TEXT. The DOS directory could be used for storing the necessary DOS commands; the PRG directory could be used for storing the word processor itself; and the TEXT directory could be reserved for all text files.

• Increased efficiency. Subdirectories save a lot of work. Let's assume you have the word processor disk described above, and it's almost full. You want to delete all of the text files, but nothing else. If you have a TEXT subdirectory, you would just enter the following to delete all the files in the TEXT directory of the disk in drive A:

```
CD A:\TEXT<Enter>
DEL *.*<Enter>
```

This command only affects the files in the TEXT directory.

<table>
<tr><td>**7.2.7**</td><td>## Copying files</td></tr>
</table>

Now we get to the practical application of the subdirectories. First of all, we need a file. Make sure the DIR_WORK disk is in drive A:. Enter the following to make sure that the root directory is the current directory:

```
CD A:\<Enter>
```

Use the COPY CON command to write the following letter to Gary. Enter the following:

```
COPY CON LETTER.TXT<Enter>
Dear Gary,<Enter>
<Enter>
Thank you very much for the birthday gift. I hope<Enter>
you'll drop in soon. We can have a belated<Enter>
birthday party. Please call me before you come.<Enter>
<Enter>
Sincerely,<Enter>
Bob<Enter>
<F6><Enter>
```

When you invoke the DIR command, you will find the file LETTER.TXT in addition to the three subdirectories. The directory should look something like this:

```
Volume drive A is DIR_WORK
Directory of A:\

GARY          <DIR>      3-09-89  3:23p
WILLIAM       <DIR>      3-09-89  3:23p
LARRY         <DIR>      3-09-89  3:23p
LETTER    TXT      179   3-09-89 11:50a
         4 File(s)   346112 bytes free
```

The file is now available for testing, but it's stored in the wrong directory (the root directory). Let's copy it to the P R I V A T E subdirectory of the GARY directory, using the necessary disk pathname.

Enter:

```
COPY A:\LETTER.TXT A:\GARY\PRIVATE
```

The line you just entered tells the PC to copy the file LETTER.TXT from the root directory of drive A: to the PRIVATE subdirectory, which is in the GARY subdirectory. Assuming that the root directory was still the current directory, you could also have entered:

```
COPY LETTER.TXT A:\GARY\PRIVATE
```

Let's check to see if the file was really copied to the right place. Enter:

```
CD GARY<Enter>
CD PRIVATE<Enter>
```

Use the DIR command to check whether the LETTER.TXT file has been copied to the PRIVATE directory. Your directory listing should look something like this:

```
Volume in drive A is DIR_WORK
Directory of A:\GARY\PRIVATE

.              <DIR>      3-09-89   3:23p
..             <DIR>      3-09-89   3:23p
LETTER    TXT       179 3-09-89 11:50a
        3 File(s)   345088 bytes free
```

Now enter the following to copy this file to the WILLIAM directory. Enter one of the following (not both—either one does the same job):

```
COPY A:\GARY\PRIVATE\LETTER.TXT A:\WILLIAM<Enter>
COPY LETTER.TXT A:\WILLIAM<Enter>
```

Now check if the copying procedure was successful. We can move relative to our present location using periods:

```
CD ..<Enter>
CD ..<Enter>
CD WILLIAM<Enter>
```

Enter the DIR command. Your directory should look something like this:

```
Volume in drive A is DIR_WORK
Directory of A:\WILLIAM

.              <DIR>        3-09-89    3:23p
..             <DIR>        3-09-89    3:23p
LETTER   TXT        179    3-09-89   11:50a
         3 File(s)   344064 bytes free
```

You can also use paths to move quickly from directory to directory. Enter the following to return to the PRIVATE directory:

```
CD A:\GARY\PRIVATE<Enter>
DIR<Enter>
```

You'll see that you're now in the PRIVATE directory again. Now enter the following to return to the WILLIAM directory:

```
CD A:\WILLIAM<Enter>
```

7.2.8   Deleting subdirectories

Now for a few words about deleting subdirectories. If you use the DEL command, it appears to work because DOS doesn't return any error messages. Enter:

```
CD A:\GARY<Enter>
DEL *.*
```

DOS will probably ask if you're sure you want to do this. Press <Y><Enter>. When the prompt returns, enter the following:

```
DIR<Enter>
```

The PRIVATE directory still exists. Enter:

```
CD PRIVATE<Enter>
DIR<Enter>
```

The LETTER.TXT file is still in the PRIVATE directory.

The developers of DOS built in a number of safety factors. If you requested a mass delete of all files from the root directory (i.e., DEL *.*), the system asks if you want all files deleted. Even if you press <Y><Enter>, the DEL *.* command only deletes files from the current directory. Any subdirectories on the disk, and their files, remain intact.

There are two methods available to delete all files in a subdirectory:

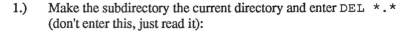

1.)   Make the subdirectory the current directory and enter DEL *.* (don't enter this, just read it):

```
CD A:\WILLIAM
DEL *.*
```

2.)   Change to the next higher directory and enter the name of the directory (don't enter this, just read it):

```
CD A:\
DEL WILLIAM
```

Both the above command sequences delete the contents of the WILLIAM directory only.

7.2.9   Removing a directory

The RD (also called RMDIR—both are abbreviations for Remove Directory) command deletes an *empty* directory from memory. Enter:

```
RD GARY<Enter>
```

The screen displays the following or a similar message:

```
Invalid path, not directory,or directory not empty
```

This message means that either the path is wrong, the name is not a directory, or the directory still contains data. We must first delete any files and additional directories from the GARY directory before we can delete the GARY directory itself. Enter the following:

```
CD A:\GARY<Enter>
RD OCCUP<Enter>
CD PRIVATE<Enter>
```

This sequence moves you into the GARY directory, removes the OCCUP directory, and then moves you to the PRIVATE directory. Continue:

```
DEL *.TXT<Enter>
CD ..<Enter>
RD  PRIVATE<Enter>
CD ..<Enter>
RD GARY<Enter>
```

This sequence removes all files with a .TXT extension, removes the PRIVATE directory, changes to the main directory and removes the GARY directory.

Summary
The RD command removes the specified empty directory from the specified disk. You cannot use RD unless all data is removed from the directory you want removed.

7.2.10   File copy verification

Some error messages may occur when you try copying from subdirectories to subdirectories. Here are some of these error messages.

•   While copying files, keep in mind the number of files that were actually copied. If you gave the wrong source file or its path, DOS responds with this or a similar message:

```
File not found
```

•   If you provided the wrong destination path, DOS responds:

```
0 Files copied
```

This could be a crucial error if you wanted backup copies of important files on another disk. However, if the original files couldn't be found, no files are copied to the backup disk.

Paths & copies During copying, all you really need to give for a destination is the path to the subdirectory to which you want the file copied. If you want the file stored under another name, then you must include the name, separated from the path by a backslash. Here's the process in detail.

Enter:

```
COPY A:LETTER.TXT A:\WILLIAM<Enter>
```

This process copies the file LETTER.TXT under the same name to the WILLIAM directory. Now enter:

```
COPY A:LETTER.TXT A:\WILLIAM\LETTNEW.TXT<Enter>
```

This process copies the file LETTER.TXT to the WILLIAM subdirectory under the name LETTNEW.TXT.

7.2.11   Multiple disks and current directories

For every connected drive, DOS remembers the current directory. In other words, if you change drive specifiers, then change drive specifiers back to the original, you'll still be in the same directory level that you were when you started.

Make the following preparations:

Single-drive: Make sure the DIR_WORK disk is in drive A:.

Hard disk: Make sure the DIR_WORK disk is in drive A:.

Dual-drive: Make sure the DIR_WORK disk is in drive A:. Place any formatted disk in drive B: (e.g., BACKUP SYSTEM).

Enter the following:

```
A:\<Enter>
PROMPT $P$G<Enter>
MD GARY<Enter>
CD GARY<Enter>
MD PRIVATE<Enter>
CD A:\GARY\PRIVATE<Enter>
B:<Enter>
MD RALPH<Enter>
CD B:\RALPH<Enter>
A:<Enter>
B:<Enter>
```

PROMPT $P displays the current directory. As you switch between A: and B:, you can see that MS-DOS recalls the current directory path.

Now let's copy the file LETTER.TXT from the root directory to the PRIVATE directory of drive A:. Enter:

```
COPY A:\LETTER.TXT A:\GARY\PRIVATE<Enter>
```

Now let's copy the LETTER.TXT file from the PRIVATE subdirectory to the RALPH directory of drive B:.Enter:

```
COPY A:\GARY\PRIVATE\LETTER.TXT B:\RALPH<Enter>
```

We can achieve the same effect with:

```
COPY A:LETTER.TXT B:<Enter>
```

You might have assumed that LETTER.TXT from the root directory of A: would be copied to the root directory of B:. Not at all—the copy process documented here copies the file from the *current directory* of drive A: to the *current directory* of drive B:.You will soon get used to this capability and save much work.

There is a possibility of errors occurring. Assume you selected the directories for both drives as in our example, and now wanted to copy the file from the root directory of A: to the root directory of B:. You entered:

```
COPY A:LETTER.TXT B:<Enter>
```

You might get one of these error messages:

```
File not found
0 files copied
```

If this occurs, check your current directories. You can avoid the error completely when dealing with root directories by using backslashes:

```
COPY A:\LETTER.TXT B:\
```

7.3   The PATH command

The PATH command is an important tool when working with directories and subdirectories. For example, suppose the DOS disk containing the transient DOS commands is in drive B:. If you need the CHKDSK command, but the current drive is A: and the selected directory is A:\GARY\PRIVATE, you won't be able to access the CHKDSK command from the PRIVATE directory. DOS would simply respond:

```
Bad command or filename
```

The PATH command tells DOS where to look for any DOS commands and programs. For example, if you entered:

```
PATH B:\
```

DOS would look in drive B: for the CHKDSK command. If the DOS disk is always in drive B, this PATH command could be incorporated into the AUTOEXEC.BAT, so that DOS would automatically look in drive B: (or whatever drive) for DOS commands.

This capability is even more important for hard disk system users. Most systems are configured with a DOS subdirectory in drive C:, where the system can find DOS commands. We suggest you look in your hard disk using DIR C: to see if you have a DOS subdirectory on the hard disk. If you do, **don't change anything.**

PATH has certain parameters, just like the DIR command:

Entering PATH without additional parameters displays the current path.

PATH can permit the definition of several search paths or more specific target areas. Each area must be separated by a semicolon. For example, the following PATH defines the DOS directory and the WORD directory on drive C: of this system. Command searches begin at the DOS directory. If the DOS directory doesn't contain the desired command, the search continues at the WORD directory:

```
PATH C:\DOS;C:\WORD
```

PATH ; deletes a path definition.

8.   Tricks and tips

The last seven chapters have taught you many of the concepts essential to using MS-DOS. This chapter shows you a few extra commands, tricks and items that will make your sessions with MS-DOS more efficient and more productive.

If you want more in-depth information on the data covered in this chapter, we recommend any one of the books covering advanced use of MS-DOS, or the MS-DOS Program Reference Guide from Abacus.

You'll need the following for this chapter:

•   The DOS_WORK disk

•   Two or three blank disks

•   Labels, felt-tip pen, write protection, etc.

8.1   The RAM disk

If you have a PC with only one drive, you found that you had to change disks frequently while working through the exercises in this book. Transient commands such as FORMAT and DISKCOPY can be especially troublesome, because the PATH command did not have a destination for the search path.

Thanks to MS-DOS and some brilliant programmer, we can offer you a second drive at no cost. A program on the DOS system disk allocates a certain amount of memory in the computer to act as a RAM disk. You can read data from this RAM disk, write to it, copy to and copy from it. The main disadvantage it has lies in its temporary nature. That is, once you turn the computer off, data stored on the RAM disk is gone, unless you copied that data to a disk before turning off the computer.

Make a copy of your DOS_WORK disk using the DISKCOPY command. Name this disk DOS_RAM, and be sure to label it. Now insert the DOS_RAM disk in drive A:. We want you to look for the RAM disk file for your system. Different versions of DOS have this file under different filenames: VDISK.SYS, RAMDRIVE.SYS or RAMDISK.SYS. Enter each of the titles below—one of these names will appear in the directory, so that's the file we'll access:

```
DIR VDISK.SYS<Enter>
DIR RAMDRIVE.SYS<Enter>
DIR RAMDISK.SYS<Enter>
```

As soon as you find the correct file, enter the following to edit the file named CONFIG.SYS:

```
EDLIN CONFIG.SYS<Enter>
```

Enter:

```
L<Enter>
```

A listing similar to this will appear (if yours is different, don't panic):

```
COUNTRY = 001
BUFFERS = 10
FILES = 20
DEVICE = ANSI.SYS
```

Leave these lines alone. Count the lines. Add 1 to the last line number listed. Enter this added line as the n in the command below:

```
nI<Enter>
```

When the new line number appears, enter **one** of the following, depending on the program equipped with your system:

```
DEVICE=\VDISK.SYS 200 512 64<Enter>
DEVICE=\RAMDRIVE.SYS 200 512 64<Enter>
DEVICE=\RAMDISK.SYS 200 512 64<Enter>
```

Enter the following to end the file and exit EDLIN:

```
<F6><Enter>
E<Enter>
```

Press <Ctrl><Alt><Del> to reset the computer. The following or a similar message appears on the display screen:

```
VDISK Version 3.2 Virtual drive C:
   buffer size 200 KB
...Sector size 512
   Directory entries 64
```

This message means that your PC has essentially created a disk drive. More accurately, the PC *thinks* it has an additional disk drive.

The RAM disk program allocates (reserves) a selected area of RAM in your computer. In this case, the program reserves 200 kilobytes for use as a RAM disk. If you have a PC with two drives, the RAM disk carries a drive specifier of C:. If you have a hard disk drive, which always has the designation C:, the RAM disk probably carries a drive specifier of D:.

From now on we will assume that the PC has one drive. Owners of other configurations should change the drive designations accordingly.

You can check the directory of this second drive with:

```
DIR C:<Enter>
```

It responds with the message:

```
Volume in drive C is VDISK  V3.2
Directory of C:\

File not found
```

To test the practical use of this second drive, copy the FORMAT command into the drive. Enter:

```
COPY A:FORMAT.* C:<Enter>
```

When you enter DIR C: again, this or a similar message appears:

```
Volume in drive C is VDISK  V3.2
Directory of C:\

FORMAT   COM    11474   5-28-86  12:00p
        1 File(s)     189440 bytes free
```

Remove the DOS_RAM disk from drive A:. Insert a new, unformatted disk into drive (A). Enter the following to format the disk in drive A:

```
C:<Enter>
FORMAT A:<Enter>
```

We mentioned earlier that the RAM disk is only temporary. Switch the PC off for ten seconds. Insert the DOS_RAM disk in drive A: and switch the computer on again. Enter:

```
C:<Enter>
DIR<Enter>
```

You'll see that whatever data you had in the RAM disk is now lost.

You can configure the AUTOEXEC.BAT file on your DOS_RAM disk to copy important transient commands onto the RAM disk for easy access. Enter the following command sequence, and make sure that the DOS_RAM disk is in drive A:

```
COPY CON A:AUTOEXEC.BAT<Enter>
ECHO OFF<Enter>
PROMPT<Enter>
VER<Enter>
ECHO ON<Enter>
COPY A:EDLIN.COM C:<Enter>
COPY A:FORMAT.COM C:<Enter>
COPY A:DISKCOPY.COM C:<Enter>
COPY A:CHKDSK.COM C:<Enter>
COPY A:LABEL.COM C:<Enter>
COPY A:SORT.COM C:<Enter>
DATE<Enter>
TIME<Enter>
<F6><Enter>
```

The DATE and TIME commands appear at the end, so the computer has finished processing all commands. Press <Ctrl><Alt><Del>. Once the computer finishes booting, enter DIR C: to see the directory. It should look something like this:

```
Volume in drive C is VDISK  V3.2
Directory of C:\

EDLIN    COM     7639   3-12-89  12:00p
FORMAT   COM    11474   3-12-89  12:00p
DISKCOPY COM     6346   3-12-89  12:00p
CHKDSK   COM    10379   3-12-89  12:00p
LABEL    COM     2394   3-12-89  12:00p
SORT     EXE     1914   3-12-89  12:00p
        6 File(s)    159744 bytes free
```

Create a path to drive C with:

```
PATH = C:<Enter>
```

All the commands listed can now be addressed directly from drive C:.
This overcomes a big disadvantage of a PC with only one drive by
simplifying your work. The latest change is stored permanently into
the AUTOEXEC.BAT file.

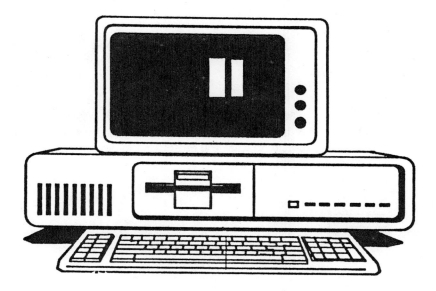

8.2   Creating boot disks

You now know all the important DOS commands and how they work with finished programs such as a word processor. Even if you are still working only with EDLIN, it would be helpful to have everything on one disk for certain applications. Until now, you could create a disk that could start your PC with only DISKCOPY. To get some space on this disk for files and maybe a word processing program, you would have to do a lot of deleting with the DEL command. However, this would require a lot of work.

We will now show you how to copy the files your computer needs to boot (start) to a new disk. The computer will then be able to start from this disk.

First we need a small added option on the FORMAT command. Remove any disk other than the BACKUP SYSTEM disk from drive A:. Insert the BACKUP SYSTEM disk in drive A:. Press <Ctrl><Alt><Del> and do what you must to get to the system prompt.

Enter:

```
FORMAT A:/S<Enter>
```

Unlike the normal FORMAT command, this one takes longer to load. The following or a similar message appears:

```
Insert new Disk in drive A:
press <Enter>
```

Remove the BACKUP SYSTEM disk from drive A:, and insert a blank disk. Press <Enter>.

After some time the following message appears:

```
Formatting completed
System files transmitted
    362496 Bytes total storage capacity
     69632 Bytes used by System
    292864 Bytes of Volume available
```

A glance at the directory shows the following or similar data:

```
Volume in drive A has no name
Directory of A:\

COMMAND   COM    24380    5-28-86  12:00p
        1 File(s)     292864 bytes free
```

The COMMAND.COM file can't take up that much memory. Examine the disk closer. The system has two "hidden" files besides the COMMAND.COM file. These files will not be discussed in detail here. All you need to know for now is that these two hidden files are important for starting the PC from scratch.

You may now copy frequently used DOS commands onto this new disk; perhaps the AUTOEXEC.BAT file you created on the DOS_RAM disk in Section 8.1; your word processor; and text files.

8.3   Batch file applications

Remember that you can execute the AUTOEXEC.BAT file without a warm or cold start. In fact, you can execute any batch file from the system prompt just by entering the filename and pressing the <Enter> key.

This provides us with an outlet for saving us time and effort. We'll start with a simple example. As you've already noticed, certain commands in MS-DOS require a lot of typing. These same commands can be written into a batch file that has a short, easy to remember name.

Let's assume you frequently use the command DIR | SORT to sort the directory, and that your hand has trouble easily reaching the pipe character on the keyboard. Entering the following creates a simple batch file to solve the problem:

```
COPY CON A:DS.BAT<Enter>
ECHO OFF<Enter>
CLS<Enter>
ECHO Now sorting files... please wait<Enter>
DIR A: | SORT<Enter>
<F6><Enter>
```

Once you close the file, the two-character command DS is available. Enter:

```
DS<Enter>
```

The batch file sorts and displays the sorted directory of drive A:.

Now, let's create a batch file that automatically formats a disk and includes the necessary data used for booting. This gives us a universal program that will make disks for our own applications (e.g., word processors, databases, etc.).

We could type these commands in one by one, but why bother? Writing a batch file saves time and effort, and saves our typing in the commands later. Insert the DOS_WORK disk in drive A: and enter the following:

```
COPY CON A:BT.BAT<Enter>
FORMAT B:/S<Enter>
COPY A:AUTOEXEC.BAT B:<Enter>
CHKDSK B:<Enter>
<F6><Enter>
```

This is a practical example of a useful batch-file. Your imagination is your only limit for creating batch files. The number of batch files you create is limited only to your memory and their visibility.

Use caution when adding commands such as FORMAT to a batch file. If you don't program these carefully, you may accidentally format a disk you didn't want formatted.

We hope that this chapter provided you with some motivation to experiment with MS-DOS.

9.   Error messages

You've seen so far that the PC is a useful tool that provides you with many capabilities. However, a PC is also very demanding. We mentioned in the second chapter of this book that the computer is a very dumb machine. It responds to what it understands, and nothing else. This means that it does what it's told, if possible, and not what the user means.

As humans, we make mistakes. Most people suffer some stress when they find themselves learning about any computer for the first time. In the heat of this stress, the beginning user can make some errors that he or she may not know how to fix, or if the errors can be fixed at all. Other errors can be caused by typing errors.

If you get an error, don't panic. Both beginning and expert users alike make mistakes and invoke errors. Keep this in mind, and stay calm as you try to figure out what went wrong.

This chapter lists some of the most common errors in MS-DOS, and how you can correct these errors as they happen.

The numbering system used on these errors has nothing to do with MS-DOS standards. We chose this numbering because we felt that these were among the "top ten" errors that occur.

Error 1   Problems occur during the booting process. This can also be caused by the lack of DOS disks. Some very inexpensive PC systems don't include operating system disks with the package, and make you buy DOS separately. Some PCs actually have MS-DOS built into a chip in the system, so the disk problem may not be an issue here.

After you switch on the PC, the messages we described earlier do not appear on the screen. Instead, another message, similar to this one, appears:

```
No System Disk or Disk error
Replace and press any key
```

Check the following for potential error sources:

1.) Did you insert one of the two disks included in the package? Were there disks with the package?

2.) Did you close the disk drive lever (5-1/4" format) or press the disk into the drive until it locked into place (3-1/2" format)?

3.) If you did both 1) and 2), try the other disk that came with your PC. Normally only one of the two disks can be used as a system disk (watch for a label such as System disk, Disk 1, etc.).

4.) Did you buy a PC with a hard disk? If you did, maybe you didn't get disks in the package. If this is the case, the contents of the disks may already be on the hard disk. Switch on the computer again, but do not insert a disk. The message we described, or a similar one, should appear.

Hard disks often come from the dealer with DOS pre-installed. You should check which directory contains your DOS commands (see Chapter 7 for information on checking subdirectories).

Error 2   You want to execute a command, but the PC returns the following or a similar message:

```
Not ready error reading drive A
Abort, Retry, Fail?
```

This means that MS-DOS can't read the disk in drive A:. Check for the following as potential error sources:

1.) Maybe this disk was unformatted. Press the <A> key to abort. Enter a DIR command, or even a VOL command to check for a directory or a volume name. If the disk was not formatted, it will repeat the message. Press the <A> key to abort. Remove the disk and insert a copy of the DOS disk. Enter:

```
FORMAT A:<Enter>
```

Follow the instructions for formatting the disk.

2.) Another thing to check: Is the disk drive lever closed, or is the disk firmly in place (depending on your disk format)? Make sure and press the <R> key to retry.

Error 3

You enter a command, but the PC doesn't react.

Check the following for potential error sources:

1.)   Did you press the <Enter> key after entering the command? In most cases, this key must be pressed before the PC executes a command. This is also true when you create a file with COPY CON and want to close the file. You must press <Ctrl><Z> or <F6> to close the file, then press <Enter> to return to the system prompt. Try pressing <Enter> first.

2.)   If, after pressing the <Enter> key several times, the PC still does not react, you may have accidentally pressed <PrtSc> to print the current screen to the printer. Turn on the printer to see what happens.

3.)   If neither 1) nor 2) worked, insert a DOS disk and warm start the PC by simultaneously pressing the <Ctrl>, <Alt>, and <Del> keys. Then try entering a command when the system prompt appears (remember to press <Enter> at the end of the command).

Error 4

You enter a command as it appears in this book. Your PC displays the following or a similar message:

```
Bad command or wrong filename
```

Check the following for potential error sources:

1.)   If the command is a DOS command, it may be a transient command. If you insert a disk that doesn't contain the command then invoke the command, the PC will attempt to load the command from disk. The above error message appears if the PC cannot locate the command. Remove the disk currently in drive A:. Insert a DOS disk in drive A:. Make sure the system prompt reads A>. Try the command again.

2.)   If the command is not a DOS command, then it must be a program name. Check the following:

•   Is the disk containing the program in the proper drive? Check the drive specifier (look at the system prompt).

•   Are you in the correct directory or subdirectory path for access? Check the directory by displaying it with CD.

3.)   If neither 1) nor 2) worked, then perhaps you mistyped the command. Compare it with the word as it appears in this book, or with the program name as listed in the disk directory. In particular, pay attention to spaces. If you invoke the directory command for drive A:, make sure it reads:

```
DIR A:
```

and not:

```
DIRA:
```

4.)   Check your version of DOS using the VER command. Some DOS commands are only available on DOS versions 3.0 and above.

Error 5   You enter FORMAT A: by mistake. The command loads from the system disk in drive A:, and the system prompts for the disk in drive A:. However, you don't want to format the DOS disk, and you don't have a blank disk handy for formatting. Remove the disk from drive A: and press <Ctrl><C>. The following should appear on the screen:

```
^C
A>
```

Pressing <Ctrl><C> terminates the FORMAT command.

Error 6   You enter a line from this book several times, but the PC always responds with an error message. You have read all the error corrections in this chapter but the error remains. It's possible that a typographical error occurred in this book. Please check Chapter 10 (Glossary) for correct names and descriptions. If Chapter 10 lists a different command from that in the problem chapter, use the Chapter 10 version and see what happens.

Error 7   You wrote a long file and want to examine it with:

```
COPY Text CON
```

This works well but you cannot stop the text output on the screen. You tried pressing <Ctrl><C>, but that key combination has no effect. After some time the PC starts to beep and the screen blinks.

Either wait for the text display to end, or press <Ctrl><Alt><Del>. When the system prompt appears, enter:

```
BREAK ON<Enter>
```

Try the COPY Text CON command again. Now you should be able to terminate the output by pressing <Ctrl><C>. Add this command to your AUTOEXEC.BAT file if necessary.

Error 8

You have two drives and have created several subdirectories. After copying a file from drive A: to drive B:, now you can't find it.

The PC has probably copied the file to a completely different directory.

Check the following for potential error sources:

1.)   You probably selected a subdirectory as a current directory and wanted to copy into the root directory. Remember that using the following command doesn't guarantee that the PC will read from or write to the root directory of either disk:

```
COPY A:FILENAME B:
```

To be certain that the copy occurs from one root directory to the other root directory, use backslashes to return to the root directory:

```
COPY A:\FILENAME B:\
```

2.)   Test which directories are active on each drive. You can do this using one of two commands:

```
CD
PROMPT $P
```

The PC will then display the valid directory for the current drive. If you enter the drive specifier (e.g., A:), DOS accepts this as the valid directory for this drive.

10.   Glossary

The following glossary for the MS-DOS operating system should be helpful when you need a fast, short support section. It is constructed to answer as many questions as possible. Cross references help lead you to other information quickly.

The glossary is designed for the person currently going through this book step by step, and needs a fast definition of an unfamiliar word or phrase. This chapter serves as a quick reference if a command or definition must be found in a hurry.

It can also be a source of information once you have some expertise in MS-DOS. The glossary can be used as a handy reference, instead of digging through the entire book to find one command definition.

The main goal of this glossary is easy comprehension. Some of the definitions given here are much simpler than they could be. If you want more detailed reference information, please read the MS-DOS Program Reference Guide from Abacus. If your interest is more in technical information (e.g., how data is stored on a disk), there are a number of fine books on the technical aspects of the PC on the market.

\<Alt\>	This key is one of the special keys on the PC keyboard. The \<Alt\> key is used in conjunction with the numeric keypad to create characters not readily available on the PC keyboard. For example, you can print the pound sign (£) on the screen by pressing and holding the \<Alt\> key, pressing \<1\>\<5\>\<6\>, then releasing the \<Alt\> key. Graphic characters are also available through the \<Alt\> key and the numeric keypad.
Application	A program designed for a specific purpose. Word processors, spreadsheets and databases are applications.
Arrow keys	The keys which move the cursor in the four possible directions. Most of the time these keys are arranged in a group on the keyboard and the arrows correspond to the direction of the movement.
ASCII	Acronym for American Standard Code for Information Interchange. ASCII is the standard for keyboard character codes, which applies to some extent to keyboards and printers. The ASCII standard covers key codes 0 to 127; individual computer manufacturers assign their own characters to codes 128 to 255 (see Byte).
Asterisk	see Wildcard

AT

Acronym for Advanced Technology. The AT is essentially the "big brother" of the PC. It has a more powerful microprocessor, a higher processing speed in most cases, larger memory capacity beyond the 640K limit set by the old PC configuration, and higher disk storage capacity.

AUTOEXEC.BAT

Abbreviation for AUTOEXECute BATch file. AUTOEXEC.BAT is a text file containing a series of commands stored in a group. Immediately after you switch on the PC, the computer searches for an AUTOEXEC.BAT file. If one exists, the commands in this file execute automatically. AUTOEXEC.BAT commands often include the display of the version of DOS in use (VER), the DATE and TIME commands. The AUTOEXEC.BAT file is a special form of batch file. Like all other batch files, AUTOEXEC.BAT can also be called and executed direct from the system prompt.

Backslash <\>

A character found on most PC keyboards. If you don't have a backslash on your keyboard, you can create it by pressing and holding the <Alt> key, and pressing <9><2>. When you release <Alt> the backslash appears on the screen. The backslash holds great importance when dealing with disk directories and subdirectories, because of its influence on the disk path (i.e., directories are separated from one another in DOS commands by backslashes).

<Backspace>

Key used for editing lines; often marked on the keyboard as <Backspace> or as <⇐>. <Backspace> allows corrections to the current line of text, as it deletes characters to the left of the cursor.

Backup copy

Duplicate of an original disk or file. Making backup copies is a good habit to get into, since data on a disk can be accidentally destroyed. See DISKCOPY for information on making backup disks, and COPY for information on making backups of files.

Bad command

Sometimes appears as Bad command or filename. Error message which indicates that the computer did not understand the input from the keyboard. It can mean, for example, that it does not know the command (perhaps you entered DIE instead of DIR) or the command could not be found on the current disk (transient commands such as FORMAT must be loaded from disk). It is also possible that the name of the file was entered incorrectly (e.g., WORS instead of WORD).

In the case of FORMAT and other transient commands such as DISKCOPY and LABEL, the simplest solution to the problem is to send the command to drive B:, where the disk to be acted on is located, instead of the current drive A: where the DOS disk is located. A sample command appears as follows (drive A: is the current drive):

```
FORMAT B:
```

Another solution is to insert the DOS disk and load in the command. Change to the required disk when prompted by the system. In the case of DISKCOPY this is a necessity, because the available disk drives are needed for the source and target disks.

BASIC
Acronym for Beginner's All-purpose Symbolic Instruction Code. BASIC is a programming language. Unlike application programs, which usually supply a specific solution to a problem area and cannot be changed, programming languages allow the user to solve almost any problem. Various commands can be used to construct a program to solve a problem. These programs function in a manner similar to batch files, and are executed one command after another. BASIC has become popular with users as a computer language because it is easy to learn. Many manufacturers include an implementation of BASIC when you purchase a computer.

Batch file
A file containing a collection of commands. MS-DOS executes these commands in sequence when the user enters the name of the file. Some other terms are batch processing or batch job. Batch files can be created using the COPY CON command (e.g., COPY CON FILE.BAT), the EDLIN line editor, or a word processing program. The .BAT extension must be included with any batch filename.

AUTOEXEC.BAT is probably the most frequently used batch file, since the PC executes AUTOEXEC.BAT when the user switches on or resets the computer.

Baud
The unit used to measure the rate of data transmission, e.g., when communicating with another computer by telephone. A baud is roughly equal to 1 bit per second. The term comes from J.M.E. Baudot, the inventor of the Baudot telegraph code, and was originally designed to describe the transmission capabilities of telegraph facilities.

In modern terms, the baud rate is the number of signal events (the signal for a 1 bit and the signal for a 0 bit are both "events") that take place on a communications line each second. Standard baud rates include 300 baud, 1200 baud, 2400 baud, etc.

Binary

A number system consisting of only two numbers (0,1), sometimes called bits. Unlike the decimal number system with its 10 numbers (0-9), the binary number system is better suited to the internal structure of a computer. Just as larger numbers can be composed in the decimal system, larger binary system numbers are constructed from several digits. Both number systems rely on the positional value of numbers. The numbers 0 - 9 in the 10 to the 0 power column have the value 0 - 9. The same numbers in the next column (10 to the 1 power) refer to 10 - 90, etc. In the binary system the column value increases as follows: 0, 2, 4, 8, 16, 32, etc.

BIOS

Acronym for Basic Input Output System. BIOS is the basic program which is permanently stored in the computer's memory, and is available even without an operating system disk. It performs, for example, the internal self test of the computer (counting up the memory available, and testing for connected peripherals such as disk drives). It also triggers the search for the operating system (MS-DOS) on the disk in the drive.

Bit

The smallest unit in the binary number system. It can only assume two states (0,1) and therefore store only two different pieces of information. To store a character, several bits must be combined into a byte.

Boot

The loading process which places the operating system in memory. A disk used for booting a PC must have two "hidden" files available for telling the PC to boot, as well as the COMMAND.COM file.

Bootable

A disk which can be used for booting (see Boot above).

BREAK

Interrupt capability. The execution of a program is interrupted when you press the <Ctrl> key and <C> key. In practice <Ctrl> is pressed first and kept depressed while <C> is activated. For example, the display of the directory on the screen (see DIR) can be interrupted in this manner. In many programs this interrupt capability has been disabled to permit an orderly termination of the program without loss of data. Even MS-DOS does not constantly test if this key combination was activated. If the capability is desired, enter BREAK ON. With BREAK OFF the constant testing is disabled, which increases execution speed for some programs.

Byte	A group of eight bits. While a bit can only assume two states, 0 and 1, a byte can store from 0 up to 255 conditions. Most of the time a character is stored in a byte. Therefore a byte can store up to 255 different characters. The standard ASCII character set consists of 128 characters; the additional characters generally used in PC software brings the total number of characters up to 255.
CD	Determines the current directory. The PC searches for files in this directory unless the user provides a complete pathname. For every drive a current directory can be indicated. If during file operations only the drive specifier is indicated, DOS automatically accesses the current directory.
CD ..	Moves the user one level up in the directory structure (e.g., toward the root directory).
CD NAME	With CD and a name, the subdirectory NAME becomes the current directory. The directory NAME must be available direct from the current directory, otherwise the complete pathname must be provided.
CD\	Returns the user direct to the root directory.
Centronics	Standard connection between the PC and a printer. The connection of other devices to the PC occurs through interfaces. These interfaces use standardized connectors. There are serial interfaces, in which data is sent as individual bits, and parallel interfaces, in which a byte can be transmitted simultaneously. Both interfaces have their own standards: Centronics interfaces for parallel; RS-232 interfaces for serial. Most printers are attached through the parallel Centronics interface. It has the device designation LPT1: (Line Printer 1).
Change Directory	The change from one directory to another. You can specify the position of the new directory either relative to the current one with CD .. or CD Name, or use the complete pathname (see also CD).
Chip	Complicated electronic circuitry built into a small space. The early days of electronics required huge circuits. Chips compressed this same circuitry into a single silicon chip, and made it possible to develop small computers for the home. The most important chip in the PC is the microprocessor, which does most of the basic tasks needed in a computer.

CHKDSK	Abbreviation for CHecKDiSK. A transient command (read from the DOS disk). CHKDSK A: tests the disk in drive A:, then displays the volume name of the disk, and the date and time the disk was formatted. In addition, the total capacity and the overview of the file types and number of files are displayed. CHKDSK also tells the user of any errors on the disk and asks the user if those errors should be corrected. The remaining space on the disk is also indicated. At the end of the display, two lines indicate the total memory available in the PC and how much memory space is still available to the user.
Clear screen	see CLS
Clock frequency	The speed of the processor is measured sometimes with the clock frequency. Unlike people, the processor consistently works internally at the same clock frequency. The IBM PC has a clock frequency of 4.77 mHz (megaHertz). Compatibles sometimes use higher frequencies, but higher speeds may create compatibility problems.
Clone	Another word to describe an IBM compatible computer (see IBM compatible).
CLS	Command which clears the screen. After the user enters CLS, the system prompt and the cursor appear on the upper left corner.
Cold start	Switching the computer off and on. Unlike the warm start, the cold start is the complete turning off and turning back on of the computer. The cold start is the last chance to have the computer start completely new. Since switching the computer off and on puts much stress on the electronic components, use the warm start (<Ctrl><Alt><Del>) whenever possible.
	Cold start and warm start can cause loss of data. Press <Ctrl><C> for stopping MS-DOS commands whenever possible. For stopping most application programs, press the <Esc> key.
Compatibility	Hardware and software that work together. A computer which is fully IBM compatible should be capable of executing all programs which exist for the IBM PC.
Compatible	see Compatibility

Configuration   The collection of devices which comprise the complete computer system (see Hardware). In an extended sense, the word configuration may also refer to the software integration of the devices. For example, the software configuration for serial interface operation of a printer includes the preparation of software drivers which instruct the computer to use this configuration.

Connector   see Slot

Console   The keyboard and monitor screen of the computer. Unlike other device designations (e.g., the serial port or the parallel port), the console (CON:) has different devices which can be addressed during input and output. An output to CON goes to the screen, an input from CON comes from the keyboard.

Control key   see <Ctrl>

Coprocessor   Name for electronic components (see Chips) which relieve the microprocessor of some important tasks. Increased performance can often be achieved through the use of coprocessors. For example, a math coprocessor often performs many of the math functions that can slow down the microprocessor during complicated graphic computations.

COPY   MS-DOS command used for copying files. There are three methods available for copying files:

     1.)   Copy a file from one disk to another. For example, in a case where drive A: is the drive containing the source disk, and where drive B: is the target disk, the command is:

         `COPY FILENAME B:`

         or

         `COPY A:FILENAME B:`

         The file on the second disk will have the same name as the file on drive A:.

     2.)   Copy a file to the same disk by providing a new filename after the original filename. This results in two identical files with two names on the same disk. The command is:

         `COPY OLDNAME NEWNAME`

3.)   Copy a file from one drive to another, while assigning a new filename:

```
COPY A:OLDNAME B:NEWNAME
```

During all copy processes with COPY, the old date and time assigned to the source file are retained.

COPY CON   Instructs the computer to copy data from the console (keyboard). Two forms of COPY CON exist:

COPY CON PRN turns your computer, together with the printer, into a primitive typewriter. Enter text on the keyboard and press <Enter> at the end of each line. When <Ctrl><Z><Enter> are pressed, COPY CON sends the data to the printer. The command COPY CON PRN can be terminated at any time, just like COPY CON FILENAME, by pressing <Ctrl><C><Enter>.

COPY CON FILENAME creates a file for storage on a disk. FILENAME can be any name up to eight characters in length, with an optional three-character file extension (e.g., .TXT). After entering the command, enter text on the keyboard, pressing <Enter> at the end of each line. Errors during input can be corrected with the <Backspace> key, by deleting the character and entering a new one. Pressing <Ctrl><Z><Enter> saves the file to disk. You can view the text file using the TYPE command (e.g., TYPE FILENAME). The command COPY CON FILENAME can be terminated at any time, just like COPY CON PRN, by pressing <Ctrl><C><Enter>.

If the PC does not accept any more entries from the keyboard during COPY CON, the input line is too long. In this case simply press <Enter>.

COPY FILE PRN   Copies an existing file to the printer.

Copying disks   see DISKCOPY

Copying of files see COPY

Correction	Corrections during input on the screen can be performed with the <Backspace> key. This deletes the character to the left of the current cursor position. You can also use the <Del> key, which deletes the character at the current cursor position.
	The function keys are a great help during command entry and the correction of input errors.
CPU	Abbreviation for Central Processing Unit. This is the main microprocessor of the PC; sometimes used to describe the PC's case as well.
<Ctrl>	The most important special key on the PC keyboard. It is located next to the <A> key, and produces important commands in combination with other keys (see <Ctrl> combinations).
<Ctrl> keys	Abbreviation for a key pressed in conjunction with the <Ctrl> key. MS-DOS uses the following control keys:
	<Ctrl><C> can be used to interrupt executions such as the display of the lines from a directory of a disk.
	<Ctrl><S> stops the screen display from scrolling. This is helpful when reading an extensive disk directory. Pressing <Ctrl><S> or any other key continues the scrolling.
	<Ctrl><Z> marks the end of a file during a COPY CON operation, in conjunction with the <Enter> key. When <Ctrl><Z> is entered while in the EDLIN line editor, this key combination forces a return to the command line. Pressing the <F6> key also generates a <Ctrl><Z>.
Current directory	To access a file or a directory, DOS uses the current directory. A directory can be made into the current directory by indicating the position relative to the current directory or giving the complete pathname. For the first case use the CD .. and CD NAME commands. In the second case, first the drive (letter and colon) and then the path through the subdirectories must be indicated, separated by the backslash.

Current drive	The standard drive or current drive is the drive to which all disk commands of the computer apply. Usually, and especially for systems with only one drive, this is drive A:. If two drives are available, the second drive can be selected with B:. This command can be reversed with A:. The hard disk drive can be selected with C:. The standard drive is displayed in the system prompt (see Prompt).
Cursor	A small, rectangular, blinking spot of light on the screen which marks the spot where a character can be placed from the keyboard. With the arrow keys (also called cursor keys) the cursor can be moved back and forth. In MS-DOS only a horizontal movement is permitted. In files and in BASIC programs the arrow keys can be used to move freely on the screen.
Cursor keys	See Arrow keys
Daisywheel printer	Daisywheel printers use a typewriter-like wheel. Individual letters press a letter on the paper, instead of composing the letter from a matrix of dots like the matrix printers. The quality of the printing is as good as that of a typewriter.
Databases	Application programs which allow fast access to data. Many database programs allow different sets of data to be combined into one package, permitting access to the different data sets simultaneously.
DATE	The current date can be set, displayed or changed at any time with this command. This date is important because, together with the time (see TIME), it is stored with the file during every storage process. This stored date indicates which version of the file or program is the most recent.

After the input of DATE the current system date (and day of the week) is displayed on the screen and the following or a similar message appears:

```
Input new date (mm-dd-yy)
```

This means that the right sequence of the input is month, day, year. Single digit entries are permissible such as 1 for January. Two digit entries can be made for the year (87 instead of 1987).

After you press <Enter>, the computer accepts the date. If a new date is not entered, the old date remains in effect.

DEL	Deletes files. The command DEL FILENAME deletes the file FILENAME. File extensions must be included in the filename when necessary. Wildcards can be used. The command DEL *.BAK deletes all files with .BAK extensions from the current directory. Usually these are backup files of files which are no longer needed and deleting them would create more storage space on a disk.

Use the command DEL *.* with caution. This command deletes all files on the disk or in the current directory. To remind the user to consider this drastic change in his inventory on the disk, a confirming prompt appears before the command is executed:

```
Are you sure? (Y/N)
```

When you enter <Y><Enter>, the system deletes all these files from the current directory.

Destination disk	Disk to which a file or disk will be copied (See Target disk).
DIR	Displays the directory of the disk which is in the current drive. First the name of the disk appears, if present (see VOL and LABEL). Then follows all available files with the following information: First the filename (with up to eight characters permitted), then if available an extension (maximum of three characters). This is followed by the size of the file in bytes. Finally the date and time is displayed when the file was stored. The assumption is that the correct time was available when the file was stored (see DATE and TIME).

Please note: During all copy procedures with the COPY command the date and time is accepted without change. At the end of the listing the number of files and the space still available on the disk (in bytes) is reported. If the disk contains no files, the following message appears:

```
File not found
```

In longer directories, the fast scrolling of data on the screen is hard to read. The flow of data can be interrupted by holding down <Ctrl> and pressing<S>. Pressing any key on the keyboard continues the scrolling on the display. A new stop can be made with the same key combination. Pressing <Ctrl><C> terminates the directory display.

If instead of the disk and filename, the PC reports after about twenty seconds with the message:

```
Not ready error reading drive A
Abort, Retry, Ignore
```

This could be caused by the failure to insert a disk or to properly close the drive. In this case lock the drive, or insert a formatted disk, perhaps the DOS disk, and press the <R> key. The command will be executed properly. If you press the <A> key (Abort), the computer responds with the system prompt.

Another source of an error message may be that the computer can access a disk, but finds that it was not yet formatted. Insert the formatted disk, or the DOS-disk, and strike <A>. You can then format a disk (see FORMAT A:). To print the directory, see printing the directory;.

DIR/P   Implementation of the DIR command. DIR/P displays the directory in page format. One screen's worth of directory goes to the screen and stops with a prompt. As soon as you press <Enter>, the next display page appears. If the disk name has scrolled past, it can be recalled with the VOL command.

DIR/W   Displays the directory in wide format. Only filenames and extensions are displayed. The advantage is that they are shown in five blocks arranged side by side. This ensures that you can usually read all filenames on the screen at once.

Directory   Part of a storage medium. Before the hard disk drive was commonly used, all files were stored in one directory, the root directory. Because of the large capacity of the hard disk drive, a separation into various directories became necessary. They are arranged in a tree structure where the root directory can contain files and subdirectories. Every subdirectory in turn can contain files and subdirectories. Most DOS commands act only on the current directory which can be indicated with CD.

The directory of a storage device contains important information about the stored files. Unfortunately, the command DIR does not permit the display of the complete directory with all subdirectories, but only the current directory. To obtain the complete overview of the data stored on a volume, use the DOS command TREE. We are fortunate that the DIR command only produces the display of the current directory. If the command tried to display the name of every file stored on a hard disk, this would take considerable time.

DIR|SORT   Displays the disk directory with filenames sorted in alphabetical order.
                    This command actually consists of two DOS commands. They are
                    connected by the pipe character, found on the keyboard. The DIR
                    command is a resident command. However, SORT is a transient
                    command, which means that it must first be read in from the DOS
                    disk. With the DOS disk it executes immediately. If it is used with
                    another disk, insert the DOS disk into drive A: and make it into the
                    current drive with A:. The SORT command should be related to drive B:
                    where the target disk is located:

                    DIR B: | SORT

                    (There must be a space between DIR and the drive designation) After a
                    brief waiting period for sorting, the files of the directory are displayed.
                    The files are sorted according to the alphabet which makes searches for
                    certain files easier.

DOS   see MS-DOS

DISKCOPY   Permits the complete copying of disks to make identical copies. The
                    command with a drive designation is:

                    DISKCOPY A:

                    or just DISKCOPY. The program then requests that a disk be inserted
                    into the drive.

                    For a PC with two drives, the source disk can be inserted into drive A:
                    and the target disk into drive B:. Use the command:

                    DISKCOPY A: B:

                    In both cases the DISKCOPY command must first be read in from the
                    DOS disk.

Disk drive	Disk drives are devices which permit the PC to work on the data stored on the disk. Depending on the size and type of the disks, there are drives for 5-1/4" disks and for 3-1/2" disks. The PC must have at least one disk drive built in. The usual configuration is two disks drives. Between the two disks drives that may be present, there are differences of rank. If the PC wants to read in the MS-DOS operating system, it accesses first the upper or left drive, depending on the construction of the PC. This can be seen by the lighting LCD on the disk drive. This is the main drive. Its designation is A:. The other drive is then drive B:. If there is a hard disk drive, it has the designation drive C:. If the PC has only one drive, that drive has the drive A: designation. This designation is important because with it commands and files can be assigned. Only one drive can be current. Its letter appears in front of the system prompt on the screen and is constantly displayed to the user (see drive designation).

Disk name	see LABEL and VOL

Disks	Removable data storage media. PC systems use two sizes. Traditionally and still most widely used are the 5-1/4" disks. This type of disk can store up to 360 kilobytes of data. This corresponds to about 360,000 characters of text. Converted to normal pages of text, it would hold about 180 pages. When purchasing new disks, make sure they are double sided and double density. Double sided means that the PC can write on both sides. Double density refers to the density of the magnetic material coating.

Since 1987 3-1/2" disks have gained in popularity. They have almost double the storage capacity and are more rugged and portable than 5-1/4" disks. Each type of disk requires its own type of disk drive.

Disk handling	The currently popular 5-1/4" disks are very fragile. When not in use, they should always be kept in a protective sleeve. Protecting the inner magnetic media is most important. Never touch this media or pour liquids on it.

Remove the disk from the sleeve by carefully pulling on the smooth end. Insert the end of the disk containing two small notches carefully into the throat of the disk drive. The oval opening which is about 3.5 cm should point toward the computer. The upper side of the disk is the one where the small round hole (with the magnetic material visible) is left of the large hole in the middle. The disk should be inserted until it strikes the back of the drive. The locking lever should be moved so that it locks the disk drive. On some drives this occurs in the clockwise direction and on others in the opposite direction. Only after the drive has been locked with this lever can the computer access the data stored on the disk.

Disks can be stored in special storage boxes which can be bought in various stores. Very important original disks or disks containing important data should be write protected (see DISKCOPY) and also stored in a safe place. A safe place is protected from dust and far from normal access.

DOS	see MS-DOS
Dot-matrix printer	Printer which produces characters on paper by driving a set of pins onto a ribbon, which leaves an impression of a character on paper.
Double density	Double density means that this type of disk has twice as much magnetic material for recording as a single density disk. Use double density disks only for PCs.
Double sided	A disk which is double sided can record on both sides. This is the usual case for a PC and should be remembered when buying disks.
Drive change	see Current drive
Drive specifier	The drive designation consists of a letter and the colon following. To indicate the standard drive, enter the drive specifier that pertains to it.
Drive	see Disk drive
ECHO	This command is of interest mainly in connection with the AUTOEXEC.BAT file. It serves the following purposes:

ECHO OFF suppresses command display during batch file execution.

ECHO ON enables command display during batch file execution.

ECHO Text displays Text on the screen.

Editing	Editing means creating a new file or correcting an existing file (see Editor).
Editor	A program which makes it possible to write or edit text. EDLIN can be used to edit text (see below), or any word processor can be used for the same purpose.

EDLIN   Line editor included on the DOS system disk. EDLIN is very limited, because it only permits movement within the current line while other editors permit free movement of the cursor on the whole screen.

                        Early editor programs were line-oriented because they were created to write and edit assembler or compiler code. Input on early systems was in batch mode with decks of punched cards. Each card contained a "line" of code which could not exceed 80 characters. EDLIN retains this limitation of old line editors.

Empty directory   A directory containing no files or subdirectories. When the DIR command is invoked from within an empty directory, the directory display indicates entries with one or two periods and a <DIR> identifier instead of filenames. The identifier is required by DOS. Empty directories may be removed by moving up one directory level using CD .. and entering the RD command.

<Enter>   An easily visible key, placed in about the same location on the PC keyboard as a <Return> key on a typewriter keyboard. This key can have different names: <Enter>, <Return>, <⏎>. Pressing <Enter> instructs the computer to execute the MS-DOS command currently entered at the system prompt line.

ERASE   Deletes files; an alternate name for the DEL command (See DEL). Some systems only accept ERASE, others accept DEL.

Erasing characters   see <Backspace>

Erase files   see DEL and ERASE

Extension   Any filename can have a three-character extension which is separated from the filename (a maximum of eight characters) by a period. The extensions .COM, .EXE and .BAT have special meanings in MS-DOS, but any other combination of letters can be selected for various files. There are some conventions which are observed, such as .TXT for ASCII text. The following extensions are used as shown:

                        BAK   Backup copy of a file (used by EDLIN and wordprocessors)
                        BAS   Program written in the computer language BASIC
                        BAT   Batch file
                        COM   Executable program file
                        DOC   Wordprocessing text file
                        EXE   Executable program file
                        TXT   ASCII Text file

File	Data stored under a name assigned by the user or manufacturer. Data files (e.g., programs, text, graphics, etc.) appear in the directory of a disk or hard disk drive as an entry containing the name, extension, size and date of storage.
File management	Working with data. Related information is stored in a data set and these are presented in sorted format. An address file is a simple form of file management.
File structures	The type and method of storing files on a medium (see tree structure). The root directory can contain both files and subdirectories, and any subdirectory can also contain files and subdirectories.
Filename	A group of letters and numbers indicating a specific file stored in a directory. A filename consists of the filename itself, which can be up to eight characters long; and the extension, which can have no more than three characters. It is important to note that spaces are prohibited and result in error messages.

The letters from A to Z and the numbers from 0 to 9 are permitted in filenames. Some special characters such as ! # $ % ( ) & - and _ may be used. Lower case letters may be used. However, MS-DOS automatically converts these to upper case letters.

The + = : ; . , < > / and \ characters may not be used in filenames.

A filename should not contain any characters which require the use of <Alt> and input through the numeric keypad.

Besides the forbidden characters there are also groups of letters which cannot appear as filenames. Among these are: CON, AUX, COM1, COM2, PRN, LPT1, LPT2, LPT3, NUL.

Floppy disk	Popular designation of the disk drive, mainly in the personal computer field. The term is derived from the flexible property of the medium. Early disks were 8 inches square and inflexible. When the first 5-1/4" disks appeared on the market, people referred to them as "floppy disks."

FORMAT

Formatting a disk (preparing a disk for storage of data). Before the command can be used, the DOS disk must be inserted into the drive. The FORMAT command is transient, and therefore must be read from the DOS disk before it can be used.

After the command has been read from disk, the disk to be formatted is inserted in the disk drive. After the user presses a key, the formatting process begins and lasts about a minute. The screen describes the progress of the formatting.

After completion of the formatting, a prompt message asks if the process should be repeated. If the user enters <Y><Enter>, the PC asks the user to insert the disk he wants to format. If the user enters <N><Enter>, the program displays the system prompt.

If a PC has two drives, or a hard disk which contains the operating system, the FORMAT command can be issued from there. The command applies to drive B: in which the new disk has been inserted. Drive A: or drive C: (hard disk) are current:

FORMAT B:

FORMAT/S

Implementation of the FORMAT command, which formats a disk and adds the files necessary to make a system disk capable of starting the computer (booting). The /S option adds these files to a disk when used in conjunction with the FORMAT command. Example:

FORMAT A:/S

The FORMAT command must be read in first from the DOS disk.

FORMAT/V

Implementation of the FORMAT command, which formats a disk and prompts the user to enter a volume name to the newly formatted disk. Example:

FORMAT A:/V

A: can be replaced with B:. The FORMAT command must be read in first from the DOS disk.

A volume label can be assigned later using the LABEL command.

Function keys   A block of ten keys lettered <F1> through <F10>. These keys are assigned different functions, depending on the application program in use. MS-DOS uses the function keys as follows:

<F1> reproduces each letter of the most recent entry at the system prompt.
<F3> reproduces the most recent entry at the system prompt.
<F6> enters a <Ctrl><Z> when pressed.

General error   The error message displayed by the PC when it cannot access a disk drive:

```
Not ready error reading drive A
Abort, Retry, Ignore?
```

The error can be caused by the following: Failure to insert a disk into the drive; the drive is not closed or locked; or the disk which was inserted is not formatted. The best remedy is to insert a formatted disk, lock the drive and press <A> (Abort). The normal system prompt should appear.

GW-BASIC   Programming language. This BASIC is usually included with MS-DOS in most PC packages (see also BASIC).

Hard disk   A hermetically sealed disk drive which usually cannot be removed from the PC (a few newer models are removable). Hard disks have much higher storage capacity than floppy disks. 20 megabyte hard disks are common in the PC market. Recent product lines of PC clones offer even larger hard disk drives, some starting at 40 megabytes and running less than 20 milliseconds access time per byte, compared with the old hard disks which required 100 milliseconds access time per byte. Hard disks are usually built into the cabinet of the PC, and are usually very sensitive to shock and vibrations. They must be treated with care. If the disk and head come into contact, data can be lost due to a head crash.

The directory of a hard disk drive can rapidly become crowded, unless subdirectories are created. New developments include devices which operate like a hard disk drive, but permit the removal of the medium. Larger hard disks require partitioning to avoid confusion. Each of these partitions in turn can contain directories and subdirectories to organize files.

Hardcopy	The ability to redirect the current contents of the screen to a printer by pressing the <Shift> and <PrtSc> keys. Following the printout, normal work can continue on the screen.
	Also, pressing <Ctrl><PrtSc> displays data both on the screen and on the printer when the user presses the <Enter> key. To print the complete directory of a disk, press <Ctrl><PrtSc>, followed by DIR<Enter>.
	The double output of data on the screen and printer remains in effect until the user presses <Ctrl><PrtSc> to disable the double display.
Hardware	Hardware consists of the computer itself and everything that pertains to it (processor, keyboard, monitor, disk drives, hard disk). The opposite of hardware is software (see Software).
Head crash	Damage of the hard disk drive and possible loss of data through the contact between the medium and the read/write head on the hard disk drive. A shock or foreign body can cause this.
Hidden files	The two files IBMBIO.SYS (or IO.SYS) and IBMDOS.SYS (or MSDOS.SYS). These files do not appear in the directory, but are important for booting (loading the operating system and starting the PC). Space must be made for these files on the disk through a variant of the FORMAT command (see FORMAT) before they can be transmitted with the SYS command.
IBM compatible	Copies of the IBM PC/XT/AT computers, following the IBM "industry standard." If programs and hardware configurations follow the IBM standard, this allows software to work with any computer. Compatibility is a relative matter, since total compatibility is a legal problem. More and more manufacturers offer IBM compatible computers which in some ways perform more efficiently than the original. This efficiency may mean that only 95% of the software written for IBM will work on an IBM compatible computer.
Interface	Connection between a PC and the outside world. Data can be exchanged through this connection between the PC and other devices. Two interfaces of different design are used: Parallel interfaces (see Centronics interface) and serial interfaces (see RS-232 interface). If a device should be attached to the PC and a suitable interface is not available, circuit boards can be obtained which contain an interface.

Invalid dir	Sometimes appears as Invalid directory. Error message which normally indicates that the indicated directory was not found. Enter the complete pathname of the desired directory to solve it.
Invalid Pars	Sometimes appears as Invalid number of parameters. Error message usually caused by the addition of a space in the command (e.g., COPY CON MARY BEL causes this error).
Joystick	Game and cursor control device, used in lieu of arrow keys. Moving the joystick lever in the desired direction moves the cursor/object being controlled by driver software. Many joysticks have a fire button in addition. The only serious application for the joystick is in a paint program. The mouse is considered a better substitute for the arrow keys.
K	Abbreviation for Kilobyte.
KEYB.COM	Control file for key assignment of DOS Versions 3.3 and above.
KEYBOARD.SYS	Keyboard driver file for DOS Versions 3.3 and above.
Kilobyte	1,024 bytes.
LABEL	The LABEL command permits the user to add an 11-character volume label name to the disk currently in the drive. Unlike filenames, volume names may include spaces.

Since LABEL is a transient command, it must be loaded from a DOS disk. |
Languages	Reference to programming languages. The user can solve problems by writing programs that solve these problems. Popular programming languages include assembly language, BASIC, Pascal and C.
Laser printer	Printer which creates characters on paper with a special printing process involving an industrial laser. Laser printers are still very expensive (starting at $1900), almost noiseless and create very good print quality.
Make Directory	see MD
MByte	Sometimes appears as MB: Abbreviation for megabyte.

MD   Abbreviation for Make Directory (sometimes also called MKDIR). Command used to create a subdirectory in the current directory. The MD command requires a directory name up to eight characters long and an optional three-character extension.

Microprocessor   Another word for chip. When used in computer science, the term chip usually refers to the main microprocessor of the computer, which controls the basic functions.

Mouse   An alternate means of cursor control. The mouse is a small box with two or three buttons on top and a ball poking out the bottom. Moving the mouse on a table moves the cursor in the same direction on the screen. The mouse is most important for painting programs and graphic user interfaces.

MS-DOS   Abbreviation for MicroSoft Disk Operating System. This is the standard operating system from the Microsoft corporation for IBM compatible PCs. The name is not really precise since MS-DOS controls disk and program operation in the computer.

                        The BIOS (Basic Input Output System) is permanently installed in the computer. The PC only becomes usable after the MS-DOS operating system has been loaded. It consists generally of a catalog of commands which can be accessed when required. Two types of commands exist: resident and transient commands.

                        Resident commands are read into the PC memory during the initial loading of the operating system, and are always available. Among these resident commands are DATE, TIME, PROMPT, CLS, VOL and others. Transient commands must be loaded from disk before they can execute. Examples of transient commands are FORMAT and DISKCOPY.

                        MS-DOS command syntax is very important during input. Every command consists of a number of parameters—command elements which are separated by spaces. The COPY CON FILENAME command is an example of a standard three-element command (one command, two parameters). MS-DOS is not case sensitive: It doesn't differentiate between upper and lower case letters during user input.

NLQ   Abbreviation for Near-Letter-Quality: Higher print quality offered by dot-matrix printers. The printer prints a line, then reprints the same line after shifting the position of the printhead slightly. NLQ mode reduces print speed considerably.

Operating system   The program which makes the computer capable of performing basic memory and disk management tasks, and permits the user to communicate with the computer through the keyboard. The operating system can be loaded from a disk (MS-DOS), or can be stored permanently in the computer (e.g., the Tandy 1000 HX has MS-DOS built into a chip in the computer).

Parallel interface   Centronics interface, usually leading to a printer (see also Centronics interface). Parallel interfaces exchange data 8 bits at a time. LPT1: is the device designation for the first parallel interface. Additional parallel interfaces (if present) can be accessed as LPT2: and LPT3:.

Parameter   Command elements of a DOS command separated from the command name by a space. The command COPY CON FILENAME uses the command name COPY and the two parameters CON and FILENAME.

PATH   The PATH command indicates the directory where DOS should search for the resident DOS commands. Without such a path, the search is limited to the current directory. PATH without a parameter displays the path which has been set.

Pathname   Indicates the location of a file or a directory on a volume. It consists of the drive specifier and subdirectories separated by a backslash. For example, a valid pathname for a file named TEXT.TXT could be:

A:\TEXT\PRIVATE\TEXT.TXT

PC   Abbreviation for Personal Computer, which was originally an IBM product first introduced in 1981. The name indicated that IBM intended that the new computer would be used by an individual. This was quite a change from the business systems of the time, which were larger multiple user systems. From this brand name came the generic description PC. It refers to all computers which are IBM compatible (able to use programs written for IBM computers). The introduction of the IBM PC/AT product line with an 80286 microprocessor was based on the concept of sharing system resources through a local area network (LAN). One AT would act as the "file server" for several PCs. The rapid drop in hardware prices and the failure of software producers to provide viable LANs makes these new and faster computers still a personal computer.

Pipe   Character which allows chaining of DOS commands (e.g., DIR|SORT). This character is available on most PC keyboards, or can be entered by pressing <Alt><1><2><4>.

Power supply	An electrical component of the computer which prepares the electrical current of the normal house wiring for use by the circuitry of the computer, similar to the transformer used on a model train layout. The size and quality of the power supply determines how many enhancements can be added to the computer, since most of them must be connected to the power supply. For example, a small capacity power supply may only be able to handle the computer and two disk drives, but not a hard disk.
Printer	Device which places computer data on paper. An indispensable tool for computing. Everything displayed on the monitor screen is printed on paper and thus made portable. Printer types include: Daisywheel; dot-matrix and laser. A printer can be addressed through either the serial or parallel interface of the computer. The parallel (Centronics) interface is designated by MS-DOS as LPT1: or PRN:. The serial (RS-232) interface is designated by MS-DOS as COM1:.
Printing a file	see COPY FILE PRN
Printing directory	Entering <Ctrl><PrtSc>DIR<Enter> sends every line of the directory to both the screen and the printer. Pressing <Ctrl><PrtSc> disables this feature.
Printing the screen	see Hardcopy
Processor	Abbreviation for microprocessor. Most references to a microprocessor in computing refer to the main microprocessor of the computer, which controls the computer's essential internal tasks (e.g., math, data movement). In the same way that different engines determine the performance of a car, various processors determine the performance of personal computers, mostly through execution speed.
Prompt	Also called system prompt. The prompt is the character or set of characters used by the computer to indicate that it is ready to accept a command or other input. The default (normal) prompt consists of the current disk drive and a greater than character (e.g., A>). The PROMPT command allows you to change the appearance of the prompt: PROMPT Waiting for input $G The PROMPT command also accepts parameters which allow it to display the date and time.

	To return to the original condition, enter the command PROMPT without any parameters. PROMPT $P displays the current drive and directory.
<PrtSc>	A key usually located on the right side of the keyboard. To send the current screen contents to the printer, press <Shift><PrtSc>.
Question mark	Wildcard which replaces individual characters in filenames for certain commands (see Wildcard).
RAM	Abbreviation for Random Access Memory. This is memory in which data can be stored temporarily. Unlike ROM (see below), RAM can be written to and read from. The contents of RAM vanish when the computer is switched off.
RAM disk	Pseudo disk drive created in the computer's RAM with the help of a program on the DOS disk. Because it is not a mechanical device, the RAM disk allows very fast file access, but loses all data when the computer is turned off. PC users with only one disk drive will find the RAM disk extremely important. Anything can be kept in a RAM disk, provided that the files do not overstep the memory bounds set for the RAM disk.
RD	Abbreviation for Remove Directory. The RD command removes empty subdirectories from a disk. If the subdirectory is not in the current directory, the complete pathname must be provided.
Redirection	The greater than character (>) redirects data to another device from its default output device. This redirection may be done to either a file or a printer.
Redirection-file	The greater than character (>) redirects data to another device from its default output device to a file.

The command DIR > FILE stores the directory under the name FILE on the disk instead of displaying it on the screen. The file can be displayed on the screen at any time by entering the command TYPE FILE.

Redirection-printer The greater than character (>) redirects data to another device from its default output device to a printer.

The command DIR > PRN sends the directory output to the printer. This command does the same thing as pressing <Ctrl><PrtSc> to print everything that follows on the printer. DIR > PRN becomes inactive once the command finished execution.

Remove Directory see RD

RENAME Command used to rename files. After the command is a space, followed by the old filename, another space and the new filename (RENAME OLDNAME NEWNAME).

If the new name already exists on the disk, an error message appears in order to prevent a file from being accidentally overwritten. Two files with the same name can not exist in the same directory.

Renaming disks see LABEL

Renaming files see RENAME

Reset see Warm start

Resident command Commands loaded as MS-DOS boots into the memory of the PC. Resident commands are always available.

Resident commands which have been described in this book are: CD, CLS, COPY, DATE, DEL, DIR, ECHO, MD, PATH, PROMPT, RENAME, RD, TIME, TYPE, VER and VOL.

<Return> Another designation for <Enter> which originated with the <Return> key found on typewriters. This book uses the <Enter> designation.

ROM Abbreviation for Read Only Memory. ROM consists of information permanently planted on a chip (see Chip), which remains intact after the computer is switched on. When the user switched the computer on, the computer reads the information from this ROM as needed. Unlike RAM, the user cannot write to ROM (hence the name).

The BIOS (Basic Input Output System) is usually contained in ROM.

Root directory	The main directory, as found on either a floppy disk or a hard disk drive. It is the highest level directory. This root directory can be accessed by entering the drive letter, the colon and a backslash. The root directory of drive A: can be displayed with the command:

```
DIR A:\
```

RS-232 interface	Standard serial interface. Serial transfer involves the transfer of data one bit at a time.
Scrolling	A process in which the display on the screen moves lines toward the top/bottom or left/right because the screen must make room for new lines.
	If several inputs have been made on the screen and no more space remains for additional inputs, the old entries disappear at the upper screen edge. Scrolling in another direction is not possible under MS-DOS, but is common in word processing programs.
Serial interface	see RS-232-interface
Set time	see TIME
Set date	see DATE
<Shift>	Two keys on the keyboard, normally located at the left and right edges of the keyboard. Pressing a <Shift> key and a letter key results in an upper case letter.
Single density	A disk type with a very limited amount of magnetic media. Most inexpensive disks are single density. Avoid using single density disks on your PC: Use double density disks only.
Single sided	A disk which is single sided can record on only the "top" side. Most inexpensive disks are single sided. Avoid using single sided disks on your PC: Use double sided disks only.
Slot	Name for a connector inside the PC where additional circuit cards can be inserted to enhance the capabilities of the computer. Lately some PCs on the market do not have these slots, and therefore cannot be enhanced without difficulty.
Software	Computer programs, including the operating system and any drivers for peripheral devices.

SORT	see DIR | SORT
Sorting directory	see DIR | SORT
Source disk	The disk which the user wants to copy. When the DISKCOPY command is invoked, a prompt requests the source disk.
Spreadsheet	Application program, often used for accounting, calculations, data tracking, business and financial "what-if" situations. As its name implies, a spreadsheet displays a set of cells into which numerical data and characters may be entered, similar to a printed accountant's spreadsheet.
Startup	see Booting, Cold start and Warm start
Storage capacity	The quantity of data the computer can store and access internally. The PC generally has from about 256,000 up to 1,000,000 characters (256K to 1 Megabyte=1000 kilobytes) of memory capacity.
Storage media	The various devices used to store the contents of the PC's memory outside the computer. Generally these include disk drives, hard disk drives and tape drives.
Subdirectory	Refers to a relative directory stored within another directory. For example, the following path refers to drive A:, the TEXT directory, the PRIVATE subdirectory contained within the TEXT directory, and the GIFTS subdirectory contained within the PRIVATE subdirectory:
	A:\TEXT\PRIVATE\GIFTS
SYS	Transient command which allows the user to assign the medium at which DOS can find the transient DOS commands (e.g., floppy disk, hard disk or RAM disk).
	SYS copies two "hidden" files (IBMBIO.SYS or IO.SYS, and IBMDOS.SYS or MSDOS.SYS, depending on your MS-DOS version) to the assigned medium. These are not displayed in the directory but are important for booting the PC. In addition to the two hidden files, the COMMAND.COM file must be copied to the assigned medium using the COPY command.
System prompt	Characters displayed on the screen, indicating readiness for user input (see Prompt).

Target disk	The disk to receive data; sometimes called the destination disk. When copying data from one disk to another (see COPY and DISKCOPY), the disk being copied is the source disk, and the target disk is the disk receiving data.
Text editor	see EDLIN, Editor and Word processor
TIME	MS-DOS command for setting or changing the current system time. This time is important because it is stored, together with the date, during every save procedure. Because of the DATE and TIME commands, the directory display shows the user which version of a file or program is the most current.

After entering the TIME command, the current system time is displayed on the screen and a prompt requests:

```
Enter new time (hh:mm:ss)
```

Enter the time in two-digit hour:two-digit minute:two-digit second format. For example, enter 13:02:00 to set the clock for 1:02 p.m. Partial entries automatically default to zero. Pressing <Enter> makes the time entered the current system time.

Transient	Commands which must be read from the DOS disk before they can be executed. The best known and most often used of these commands are FORMAT and DISKCOPY.

Other transient commands discussed in this book are: CHKDSK, LABEL, SORT, SYS and COPY.

Tree structure	The tree structure (dendritic structure) is often used as a comparison to explain the storage of files on data medium (floppy disk or hard disk). Starting at the stem (root directory), there can be branches (subdirectories) and leaves (files). Branches can have other branches (subdirectories can include other subdirectories) or leaves (files).
TYPE	DOS command used to display a text file on the screen. Entering the following command displays the text file named FILENAME on the screen:

```
TYPE FILENAME
```

The TYPE command cannot be used in conjunction with wildcards.

User interface	The communication point between the user and the computer. In DOS, command entry occurs through the keyboard.
	Other user interfaces allow communication with the computer through the use of other input devices, such as a mouse or joystick.
Utilities	Programs that either help the programmer program more efficiently, or act as tools for helping the user in disk and file management. Some utilities optimize the performance of a hard disk, others help the user recover deleted or destroyed files.
VOL	Resident command which displays the volume name of the disk in the current drive. For example, the following command displays the volume name of the disk in drive A:

```
VOL A:<Enter>
```

If the disk has a volume name, the PC displays this or a similar message:

```
Volume in drive A: is WORK1
```

If the PC displays the following, no volume name exists:

```
Volume in drive A: has no name
```

The LABEL command allows the user to add a volume name to a labeled disk.

A disk can be named during formatting using the FORMAT A:/V command. The volume name also appears in the header of the directory. With VOL there is no problem with the display of a long directory.

Warm start	The simplest method of returning the PC to its original condition is to turn off the electric power (see cold start). However, the warm start deletes the contents of memory and restarts the system without reloading the BIOS. This means that the computer doesn't count up its memory capacity, test peripherals, etc. Pressing <Ctrl><Alt><Del> warm starts the computer.

Wildcard	Characters which can replace one or more characters in filenames, allowing multiple file access in some cases. Two possibilities exist:
	Asterisk (*): replaces any number of characters related to the command. The COPY *.TXT copies all files using an extension of .TXT. The asterisk can be at the beginning or end of a filename, or in the extension.
	The COPY *.* command copies all files from the current directory.
	Question mark (?): replaces individual characters related to the command. For example, the command DIR F??D.T?T displays a directory of all four-character filenames starting with F and ending with D, *and* three-character file extensions starting with T and ending with T (e.g., FRED.TXT, FOOD.TST, FORD.TNT). As demonstrated here, multiple question marks may be used.
	Wildcards cannot be used in conjunction with the TYPE command.
Word processor	An application program for creating and editing text files. Most word processors on the market today allow the inclusion of graphics, text formatting and more.
Write protect	Protects disks from accidental formatting or file deletion. Disks can be write protected by covering the square slot on the left side with a paper sticker (5-1/4" disks), or by moving the write protect slider (3-1/2" disks). Data can be read from this disk into the memory of the PC, but nothing can be changed on the disk. This disk and its data is protected.
XT	Designation of a PC with a hard disk drive, or a PC capable of running a hard disk drive.

Index

Beginners Series books remove the confusing jargon and get you up and running quickly with your PC.

PC and Compatible Computers for Beginners - For the absolute newcomer to personal computers. Describes the PC and all of its components in an non-technical way. Introduces DOS commands.
ISBN 1-55755-060-3 $18.95
Canada: 52072 $22.95

MS-DOS for Beginners - Describes the most important DOS commands clearly and understandably. Teaches skills required to more effectively use your PC.
ISBN 1-55755-061-1 $18.95
Canada: 52071 $22.95

Excel for Beginners - Newcomers to this powerful spreadsheet and graphics software will learn to master Excel's many features in a short while. Dec. '90
ISBN 1-55755-067-0 $18.95
Canada: 52067 $22.95

Microsoft Works for Beginners - A thorough introduction to this "all-in-one" software package. Loaded with simple, practical examples.
ISBN 1-55755-063-8 $18.95
Canada: 52070 $22.95

Ventura Publisher for Beginners* - Presents the basics of the premier desktop publishing package. Many examples and illustrations.
ISBN 1-55755-064-6 $18.95
Canada: 52074 $22.95

*Companion disk available for these books

In US and Canada add $4.00 shipping and handling. Foreign orders add $12.00 per item. Michigan residents add 4% sales tax

Computer Viruses - A High-Tech Disease
describes the relatively new phenomena
among personal computer users, one that has
the potential to destroy large amounts of data
stored in PC systems. Simply put, this book
explains what a virus is, how it works and
what can be done to protect your PC against
destruction.

Computer Viruses - A High-Tech Disease
starts with a short history of computer viruses
and will describe how a virus can quietly
take hold of a PC. It will give you lots of
information on the creation and removal of
computer viruses. For the curious, there are
several rudimentary programs which
demonstrate some of the ways in which a
virus infects a PC.

Computer Viruses - A High-Tech Disease
even presents techniques on inoculating the
PC from a virus. Whether you want to know
a little or a lot about viruses, you'll find what
you need in this book. 288 pp.

About the author; Ralf Burger is a system
engineer who has spent many years
experimenting with virus programs and
locating them in computer systems.

Topics include:

- What is a computer virus
- A short history of viruses
- Definition of a virus
- How self-manipulating programs work
- Design and function of viral programs
- Sample listings in BASIC, Pascal and
  machine language
- Viruses and batch file
- Examples of viral software manipulation
- Protection options for the user
- What to do when you're infected
- Protection viruses and strategies
- Avirus recognition program
- Virus-proof operating systems

ISBN 1-55755-043-3. $18.95
Canada: 52089 $24.95

To order, fill out this form and send to Abacus along with proper payment, or call **Toll Free 1-800-451-4319.**

Qty.	Title	Price

Name:_____

Address:_____

City:_____ State:_____ Zip:_____

Country:_____ Phone:_____/_____

MI residents add 4% sales tax	
Add $4 S/H (U.S. and Canada) or Foreign orders add $12 per item	
Check/ Money Order **TOTAL**	

Charge order to my: ☐ VISA   ☐ MC.   ☐ Am.Ex.

Card #: ☐☐☐☐☐☐☐☐☐☐☐☐☐☐☐☐   Exp. Date:_____/___/___

SEE LIST OF AVAILABLE TITLES ON REVERSE SIDE

PLEASE HELP US

So that we better understand who you are and what types of books interest you, please answer the following questions and return this prepaid card to us. **THANK YOU**

Computer:
☐ IBM/ PC or compatible   ☐ Atari ST   ☐ Macintosh
☐ Commodore 64   ☐ Commodore 128   ☐ Apple II/ GS
☐ Amiga   ☐ Other: _____

I purchase most computer books from:
☐ Retail book store   ☐ Discount book store   ☐ Mail order
☐ Retail computer store   ☐ Discount computer store   ☐ Publisher direct

I learned of this book from:
☐ Magazine ad   ☐ Book review   ☐ Recommendation
☐ Store display rack   ☐ Catalog/ Brochure   ☐ Library

Suggestions for new books:_____

This book's title:_____

Your name:_____

Address:_____

City:_____ State:_____ Zip:_____

Purchased from (Store name):_____

City:_____ State:_____ Zip:_____

☑ Available book titles for IBM/ PC and compatibles

PC BEGINNERS SERIES

☑ PC for Beginners	$18.95
☑ MS-DOS for Beginners	18.95
☑ GW-BASIC Prog'ing for beginners	18.95
☑ Microsoft Works for beginners	18.95
☑ Ventura Publisher for beginners	18.95
☑ Lotus 1•2•3 for beginners	18.95
☑ Excel for beginners	18.95
☑ Microsoft Word for beginners	18.95
☑ dBASE IV for beginners	18.95
☑ UNIX/ XENIX for beginners	18.95

PROGRAM REFERENCE GUIDES

☑ dBASE III Plus	$9.95
☑ GW-BASIC	9.95
☑ Lotus 1•2•3	9.95
☑ Microsoft Word	9.95
☑ MS-DOS	9.95
☑ Multiplan	9.95
☑ Turbo C	9.95
☑ Turbo Pascal	9.95
☑ WordPerfect	9.95
☑ Wordstar	9.95

To order call **Toll Free 1-800-451-4319.**

Abacus
5370 52nd Street S.E.
Grand Rapids, MI 49502-8107

To order, fill out this form and send to Abacus along with proper payment, or call **Toll Free 1-800-451-4319.**

Qty.	Title	Price

Name:_____

Address:_____

City:_____ State:____ Zip:_____

Country:_____ Phone:_____/_____

MI residents add 4% sales tax	
Add $4 S/H (U.S. and Canada) or Foreign orders add $12 per item	
Check/ Money Order **TOTAL**	

Charge order to my: ☐ VISA   ☐ MC.   ☐ Am.Ex.

Card #: ☐☐☐☐☐☐☐☐☐☐☐☐☐☐☐☐ Exp. Date:____/____/

SEE LIST OF AVAILABLE TITLES ON REVERSE SIDE

PLEASE HELP US

So that we better understand who you are and **what types of books interest you**, please answer the following questions and return this prepaid card to us. **THANK YOU**

Computer:
☐ IBM/ PC or compatible   ☐ Atari ST   ☐ Macintosh
☐ Commodore 64   ☐ Commodore 128   ☐ Apple II/ GS
☐ Amiga   ☐ Other: _____

I purchase most computer books from:
☐ Retail book store   ☐ Discount book store   ☐ Mail order
☐ Retail computer store   ☐ Discount computer store   ☐ Publisher direct

I learned of this book from:
☐ Magazine ad   ☐ Book review   ☐ Recommendation
☐ Store display rack   ☐ Catalog/ Brochure   ☐ Library

Suggestions for new books:_____

This book's title:_____

Your name:_____

Address:_____

City:_____ State:_____ Zip:_____

Purchased from (Store name):_____

City:_____ State:_____ Zip:_____

☑ Available book titles for IBM/ PC and compatibles

PC BEGINNERS SERIES		PROGRAM REFERENCE GUIDES	
☑ PC for Beginners	$18.95	☑ dBASE III Plus	$9.95
☑ MS-DOS for Beginners	18.95	☑ GW-BASIC	9.95
☑ GW-BASIC Prog'ing for beginners	18.95	☑ Lotus 1•2•3	9.95
☑ Microsoft Works for beginners	18.95	☑ Microsoft Word	9.95
☑ Ventura Publisher for beginners	18.95	☑ MS-DOS	9.95
☑ Lotus 1•2•3 for beginners	18.95	☑ Multiplan	9.95
☑ Excel for beginners	18.95	☑ Turbo C	9.95
☑ Microsoft Word for beginners	18.95	☑ Turbo Pascal	9.95
☑ dBASE IV for beginners	18.95	☑ WordPerfect	9.95
☑ UNIX/ XENIX for beginners	18.95	☑ Wordstar	9.95

To order call **Toll Free 1-800-451-4319.**

NO POSTAGE
NECESSARY
IF MAILED
IN THE
UNITED STATES

Abacus
5370 52nd Street S.E.
Grand Rapids, MI 49502-8107